INSIGH

GREAT BREAKS

GLASGOW

Walking Eye App

Your Insight Guide purchase includes a free download of the destination's corresponding eBook. It is available now from the free Walking Eye container app in the App Store and Google Play. Simply download the Walking Eye container app to access the eBook dedicated to your purchased book. The app also features free information on local events taking place and activities you can enjoy during your stay, with the option to book them. In addition, premium content for a wide range of other destinations is available to purchase in-app.

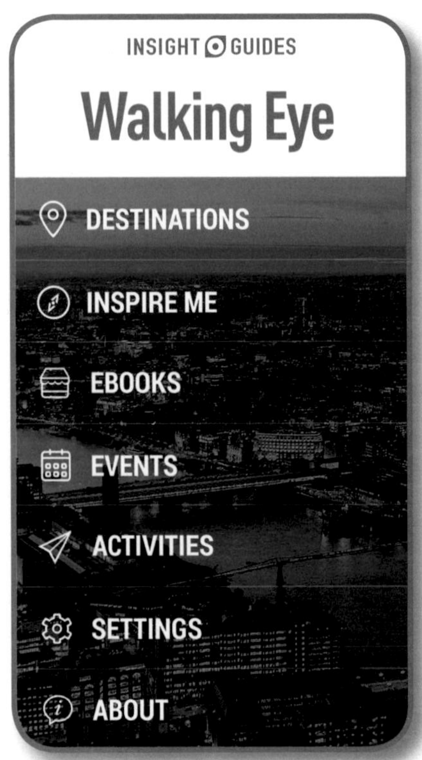

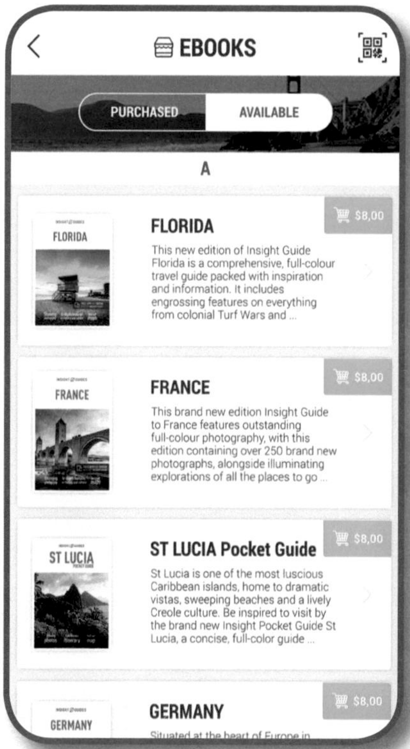

HOW TO DOWNLOAD THE WALKING EYE APP

Available on purchase of this guide only.

1. Visit our website: www.insightguides.com/walkingeye
2. Download the Walking Eye container app to your smartphone (this will give you access to your free eBook and the ability to purchase other products)
3. Select the scanning module in the Walking Eye container app
4. Scan the QR Code on this page – you will be asked to enter a verification word from the book as proof of purchase
5. Download your free eBook* for travel information on the go

* Other destination apps and eBooks are available for purchase separately or are free with the purchase of the Insight Guide book

Contents

Walks and Tours

Travel Tips

Glasgow's Top 10

From Glasgow's dazzling variety of art and architecture to the wild natural beauty of the surrounding countryside, here, at a glance, are the top sights and activities of this fascinating Scottish city

▲ **Kelvingrove Art Gallery and Museum.** Discover the wonders of Victorian civic endeavour at this red-sandstone museum filled with compelling exhibits. See page 72.

▲ **Shopping.** Choose from swanky designers at Princes Square or speciality shops in the Merchant City and West End. See pages 54, 68 and 78.

▲ **Loch Lomond and the Trossachs.** It's adventures galore in this national park, dipping into Britain's largest lake, trekking and visiting beguiling villages. See page 104.

▶ **Glasgow culture and nightlife.** With its myriad music scenes, cutting-edge theatre and nightspots, Glasgow caters for everyone. See page 12.

▲ **Cathedral and Necropolis.** Glasgow's impressive cathedral was founded in 1136, while the Necropolis provides spine-tingling moments amid crumbling temples and monuments. See pages 20 and 22.

▲ **Riverside Museum.** Glasgow's award-winning transport museum features buses, trams, trains, bikes and cars. See page 74.

▲ **Burns Country.** On the trail of the Scottish bard, visiting Alloway Kirk's graveyard, Burns Cottage and the Robert Burns Birthplace Museum. See page 110.

▼ **Pollok Estate.** A splendid mansion, riverside walks, biking trails, and the world-class Burrell Collection (closed 2016–19) make for a memorable Southside day. See page 88.

▼ **New Lanark.** David Dale and his son-in-law Robert Owen's model factory town is now a fascinating Unesco World Heritage Site. See page 109.

▼ **Glasgow arts scene.** The Gallery of Modern Art and assorted galleries give the city one of the world's most vibrant contemporary art scenes. See page 66.

The ornate façade of the Stock Exchange building.

Overview

The Art of Reinvention

Glasgow is a city continually in flux: its vibrant culture, and its grand architectural splendours of sandstone and steel make it sparkle despite dark urban realities

Glasgow is something of a Renaissance city. Like a proud fighter who refuses to be knocked down, this vibrant, bustling, rumbustious Scottish city continues to look forward. Born as a fishing village on the slopes above the meandering River Clyde, Glasgow has been, in turn, a market town, an ecclesiastical centre, a seat of learning, a city of merchant adventurers, a gateway to the New World, an industrial powerhouse of the British Empire and a European cultural capital.

ARCHITECTURE

From the southern approach to the city, first impressions are not great. Despite some misguided 1960s urban planning – Brutalist tower blocks and the M8 motorway, which rips through the heart of the city – Glasgow is an architectural treasure house. Its mix of Victorian, Georgian, Venetian and Art Deco equals anything in Europe.

The city retained its grim face until well into the second half of the 20th century, when the New Glasgow Society – a loose collection of early eco-warriors – led a rearguard action against the City Corporation's policy of 'If it's old, knock it down'. Victorian tenement homes were stripped and refurbished instead of being demolished, revealing honey-and-red sandstone wonders and striking detail. The defining moments in Glasgow's recent past were its selection in 1990 as European City of Culture and its hosting of the Commonwealth Games in 2014.

ECONOMY AND RENEWAL

The city set about reviving its fortunes with the bold regeneration of the inner-city riverbank. In 2011, the Zaha Hadid-designed Riverside Museum added to the shimmering riverside scene, along with the futuristic SSE Hydro venue, opened in 2013. Meanwhile, the Merchant City's abandoned warehouses continue to be transformed into swanky apartments, businesses and restaurants. The Trongate 103 arts centre is at the heart of a plan to regenerate run-down streets and connect the city with the Clyde, all part of the 2015 City Deal for Glasgow, a £400-million regeneration programme planned over the next decade.

Glasgow boasts some chic shopping centres, such as Princes Square, part of Glasgow's so-called 'Style Mile'. High-profile events including the biennial Glasgow International Festival continue to invigorate the city. Its reputation as a dour, violent slum is finally

The riverside is packed with striking buildings, such as the Science Centre.

being shaken off and Glaswegians are generally proud of the transformation.

LOCATION

The city lies in the wide strath, or plain, of the River Clyde and is sheltered to the north, east and south by high, open ground; it's possible to be in rolling countryside 20 minutes' drive from the city centre. Glasgow is about 26 miles (42km) from the sea at Greenock, and the Clyde starts to widen into the Firth just below the Erskine Bridge at Old Kilpatrick. North of the city, the Campsie Fells rise to 1,900ft (580m) and are dramatically visible from many areas.

CLIMATE

The Gulf Stream warms the whole of the west coast of Scotland, and Glasgow is a beneficiary of more temperate weather than might be expected from its latitude. Winters are generally mild (between 0°C/32°F and 6°C/43°F) with more rain than snow, though cold snaps of as low as -24°C (-11°F) have been known. Summers, in common with the rest of Britain, appear to be growing warmer, with temperatures of up to 25°C (77°F).

However, the prevailing westerly winds that blow across the Atlantic bring with them their fair share of rain.

The doomed ocean liner RMS *Lusitania*, pictured here in 1907, was built in the Glasgow shipyards.

The grand Merchants' House in 1874.

A day that offers glorious sunshine in the morning can become a depression of drizzle by the early afternoon. Go prepared.

HISTORY OF TURMOIL

Glasgow was inhabited as long ago as 4000BC, when hunters pushed north in the wake of the retreating ice. From around AD 71 until c.211 the Romans failed to have overall control over Scotland, and their final retreat led to centuries of turmoil between warring tribes of Scots, Picts, Britons and Angles.

St Ninian began missionary work in Strathclyde in the 4th century, but St Mungo is credited as the founder of the city in AD543, although only legend bears witness to his arrival. Glasgow Cathedral was founded in 1136 on the site of St Mungo's Church on the banks of the Molendinar, a pretty *burn* (stream). Although the city was seen as a respectable seat of learning (Glasgow University was created in 1451), with strong religious traditions throughout the Middle Ages, all the political and military action took place in Edinburgh, Falkirk and Stirling.

INDUSTRIAL AWAKENING

The British Empire spawned Glasgow's development as an important port city. Civil engineer John Gol-

The People

Glaswegians stereotypically have a way with words, even if visitors have difficulty understanding them. The patter, sociologists argue, is a mix of native sharpness, Highland feyness, Jewish morbidity and the Irish *craic* (witty story-telling). Much of Glasgow's story has been harsh, and, in the past, raising a laugh served as an antidote to adversity. The shipyards of the 1960s, for example, have provided plenty of material for Glaswegian-born comedian, Billy Connolly.

Glaswegians are generally very quick and funny.

borne's ingenious plan of the 1770s – to build piers along the banks and allow the river to scour its own bed – turned Glasgow into a serious contender as an Atlantic port.

The 'Tobacco Lords' were the first major merchants; many of their houses still stand. They created not only the tobacco trade with Maryland, Virginia and North Carolina, but a merchant class. Their need for iron tools, glass, pottery and clothes to trade with the colonies was the impetus for the city's awakening to the Industrial Revolution.

Glasgow became a cotton town in 1780. Within a decade, scores of mills were using the fast-flowing Scottish rivers to power their looms, and immigrants from Ireland and the Highlands were flooding in. Glasgow's population exploded, from 23,500 in 1755 to a peak of 1,128,000 in 1939. The metal-bashing industries – shipbuilding, ironworks, armaments – were complemented by textiles, chemicals and manufacturing.

During the 20th century, Glasgow shared in the spoils and misfortunes of the industrialised world. Recent city administrations, however, have pragmatically courted private finance to unlock the city's post-industrial potential. New developments and regeneration projects have given the city a sense of civic pride, and Glasgow looks forward to a positive future as this forward-thinking continues.

Find our recommended restaurants at the end of each tour. Below is a price guide to help you make your choice.

Eating Out Price Guide

Two-course meal for one person, including a glass of wine.

£££ = over £45
££ = £25–45
£ = under £25

Guide to Coloured Boxes

Eating
Fact
Green
Kids
Shopping
View

This guide is dotted with coloured boxes providing additional practical and cultural information to make the most of your visit. Here is a guide to the coding system.

Entertainment

PERFORMING ARTS

Glasgow is a thriving centre for the arts, mixing the old with some of Scotland's most cutting-edge scenes. When it comes to variety of music events, art shows and nightlife, few cities in Britain can compare. For full details of performance times and dates, check in the local press (*The Herald* and *The List* are the best), or visit www.visitscotland.com or www.peoplemakeglasgow.com

Theatre, dance, opera and comedy

The Citizens Theatre (tel: 0141-429 0022; www.citz.co.uk) in Gorbals Street combines iconoclastic drama with stunning design. **Tramway** (tel: 0845-330 3501; www.tramway.org) is an exciting arts centre and theatre space, home of Scottish Ballet.

The **Tron Theatre** (tel: 0141-552 4267; www.tron.co.uk) shows hard-hitting Scottish drama, concerts, comedy and pantomime. Comedians Billy Connolly and Frankie Boyle appear at **The**

Tramway is the home of Scottish Ballet.

The iconic Clyde Auditorium, popularly known as the Armadillo.

King's Theatre (tel: 0844-871 7648) in Bath Street and **Pavilion** in Renfield Street (tel: 0141-332 1846).

Scottish Opera and Scottish Ballet mount major productions at the **Theatre Royal** (tel: 0844-871 7627). Modern dance productions, musicals and plays are also staged here.

Classical music and gigs

The **Glasgow Royal Concert Hall** (tel: 0141-353 8000) hosts regular performances by the **Royal Scottish National Orchestra** (tel: 0141-226 3868; www.rsno.org.uk). The refurbished **City Halls** and the **Old Fruit Market** in the Merchant City area are home to the **BBC Scottish Symphony Orchestra** and the Scottish Music Centre (tel: 0141-522 5222). **Henry Wood Hall** (tel: 0141-225 3555), at 73 Claremont Street, is a beautiful venue in a former church, mainly used for classical events.

The **Scottish Exhibition and Conference Centre** (tel: 0141-248 3000) and the adjacent **Clyde Auditorium** – dubbed the 'Armadillo' – stage high-profile classical concerts and big rock and pop gigs. The nearby SSE Hydro (0844-395 4000) hosts international mega stars and high-profile sporting events. Jazz, blues and country gigs are held at City Halls, Old Fruitmarket and the Royal Concert Hall. For a closer look at the music scene and venues see feature, page 66.

Film

The first stop for arty, independent film is the wonderful **Glasgow Film Theatre** (12 Rose Street; tel: 0141-332 6535; www.glasgowfilm.org). Both the **Centre for Contemporary Arts** (**CCA**) and **Trongate 103** arts centres screen indie films and flicks for kids. For more mainstream releases, try **The Grosvenor** in the West End (Ashton Lane; tel: 0845-166 6002) and **Cineworld** (Renfrew Street; tel: 0871-200 2000).

NIGHTLIFE

Pubs and bars

Drinking has always been a serious business in Glasgow. For sophisticated drinking and eating head to the Merchant City. Sauchiehall Street has a reputation for being mobbed by inebriated revellers at weekends. The West End is popular with students and arty types.

Some of the best hostelries include **Babbity Bowster** (Mon–Sat 11am–midnight, Sun 12.30pm–midnight) at 16–18 Blackfriars Street, home to a heaving bar that attracts an eclectic mix of media types and local worthies, and **Blackfriars** at 36 Bell Street (Mon–Thu 11am–midnight, Fri–Sat 11am–3am, Sun 12.30pm–midnight), which has a friendly bar, a range of real ale beers and is a comedy club and music venue at night. Check out the up-to-the-minute micro-brewery Drygate at 85 Drygate (daily 11am–midnight), with excellent beer selection, sun terrace and events hall. For whisky connoisseurs, try **The Pot Still** at 154 Hope Street (daily 11am–midnight), featuring drams from around the world.

Clubs

Glasgow's club scene is eclectic. **The Arches** (253 Argyle Street, tel: 0141-565 1000) offers big-name DJs, while **The Buff** (142 Bath Lane, tel: 0141-248 1777) hosts an eclectic mix of music from indie to Motown. **The Flying Duck** (142 Renfield Street, tel: 0141-564 1450) has a sleek new look and features a Thursday night pop party, while the **Sub Club** (22 Jamaica Street, tel: 0141-248 4600) is famed for its cultish devotion and infamous dance nights.

Festivals

Celtic Connections (www.celticconnections.com) celebrates Celtic musical culture in January. The biannual **Glasgow International Festival** (www.glasgowinternational.org; Apr–May) showcases the latest visual arts. The **West End Festival** (www.westendfestival.co.uk) has lots of fun events and concerts in June. Also in June is the **Glasgow Jazz Festival** (www.jazzfest.co.uk).

The **Glasgow Comedy Festival** (www.glasgowcomedyfestival.com) is in March and the arts-focused **Merchant City Festival** (www.merchantcityfestival.com) is in July. **Pride Glasgow** (tel: 0844-664 5428; www.pride.scot), Scotland's largest Pride gay-lesbian festival, takes place over a weekend in July or August, .

Revellers in Ashton Lane at the West End Festival.

Café Smith occupies a tenement building off the High Street.

Tour 1

High Street

This half-day, 1-mile (1.6km) walk takes you from the gritty old traders' hub Mercat Cross up to the spiritual and spooky realms of the Cathedral area and Necropolis

Mercat Cross was the visible evidence of a burgh's right to hold a market, the domain of traders and merchants, making this area Glasgow's traditional centre of social and economic life for many centuries. There is no clear evidence of exactly where the original **Mercat Cross** ❶ stood, and the squat octagonal building with a unicorn-topped pillar that now stands on the intersection at Glasgow Cross is a replacement erected in 1929. The Mercat Building located behind it is, despite its Chicagoesque appearance, a warehouse erected in 1925. The arts centre Trongate 103 and the Tron theatre (see page 41) have contributed to revitalising this part of the Merchant City area.

Highlights

- Tolbooth Steeple
- Barony Hall
- Provand's Lordship
- St Mungo Museum of Religious Life and Art
- Glasgow Cathedral
- Necropolis

TOLBOOTH STEEPLE

Starting our walk here, the cross is dominated by the **Tolbooth Steeple** ❷, which lies stranded in the middle of busy traffic where the High Street passes into Saltmarket. The Tolbooth was once an integral part of civic life in Glasgow and has occupied this site in various forms since

The Tolbooth Steeple.

the earliest days. Its functions were manifold, from a meeting place for the town council, to a tax collection point, courthouse and jail.

The square tower was part of a five-storey building that extended west along the Trongate, towards the steeple of **Tron-St Mary's** (see page 41), and its buttressed crown houses the latest of a fine carillon of bells which, in the 18th century, played out a different Scottish melody every two hours. The present bells, installed in 1881, were tended by hereditary bell-ringers, the last of whom, Jessie Herbert, rang the bells until 1970. Their annual high point was marking the Hogmanay celebrations that saw vast crowds welcoming the New Year in boisterous fashion. The Hogmanay party now takes place in George Square.

HISTORICAL HIGH STREET

The High Street runs north past Victorian tenements (1883), with shops below on the left and flats converted from old warehouses on the right. The street names offer clues to the past: Blackfriars Street, from the 13th-century Dominican monastery; Bell Street, after Provost Sir John Bell (1680); and College Street, denoting the **Old College**, which was sited here until the middle of the 19th century. The University of Glasgow was established by Bishop William Turnbull in 1451 and flourished for the next few centuries in a pleasant environment between the High Street and the Molendinar Burn. It was here that Adam Smith, author of the seminal work on laissez-faire economics *The Wealth of Nations*, was appointed Professor of Moral Philosophy in 1752.

The university moved westwards in 1870 (see page 80), and the site was sold to the City of Glasgow Union Railway Company, which demolished it and erected the College Goods Station, which has now also gone. However, the area is currently undergoing substantial redevelopment.

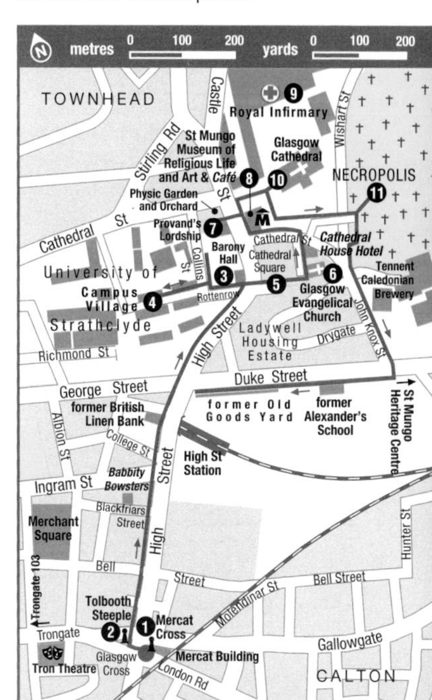

Barony Hall was designed in the Scottish Gothic Revival style and is a popular venue for weddings, as well as the site of graduation ceremonies.

On the left, opposite the High Street Station, is the shell of the old **British Linen Bank**, which has a statue of Pallas, goddess of wisdom and weaving, and a plaque on the corner recalling that the poet Thomas Campbell frequented a coffee shop on the site.

Crossing George Street and curving up the hill, the road is flanked by restored tenements with crow-stepped gables, turrets and balconies. On this hill, the Scots freedom fighter William Wallace – glorified by Hollywood and Mel Gibson in the film *Braveheart* – fought a running battle with English forces in 1297.

UNIVERSITY DIGS

On the corner of High Street and Rottenrow is **Barony Hall** ❸ (Sat–Sun), the first major building of the Cathedral complex, which opens out onto Castle Street. It was built in 1889 from beautiful red sandstone and graced with slender stained-glass windows and a grey Gothic spire. It is now owned by the University of Strathclyde, and on graduation days the street teems with begowned students and tutors making their way to the hall to receive and bestow degrees. Rottenrow is one of Glasgow's earliest streets, and its name has nev-

The Mercat Building on the Trongate.

er been adequately defined, with suggestions as far apart as *route du roi* (king's way) to *vicus ratonum* (street of rats). It leads to the university's **Campus Village** ❹, a pleasing and colourful student quarter built over the past two decades.

AROUND CATHEDRAL SQUARE

Opposite Barony Hall is **Cathedral Square** ❺, guarded by a rather imperious equestrian statue of William of Orange, which was resited by the Provincial Grand Black Chapter of Scotland in 1989 from the Trongate, where it suffered terrible indignities each Hogmanay. It is said that the tail of King Billy's horse was broken off by a reveller and replaced with a ball and socket joint, with the result that on particularly stormy days, the tail can be seen to wave in the breeze.

On the south side of the square is the 1960s Ladywell housing estate, built over the medieval well of that name and the former Duke Street jail. The east side is bounded by the **Glasgow Evangelical Church** ❻, which features life-sized statues of the Apostles. Just to the north, more worldly pleasures can be found at the **Cathedral House**, a small hotel housed in a red sandstone building dating from 1896, which has an interesting three-level bar and is reputedly haunted.

The oldest dwelling-house still standing in Glasgow is **Provand's Lordship** ❼ (tel: 0141-276 1625; www.glasgowlife.org.uk; Tue–Thu, Sat 10am–5pm, Fri–Sun 11am–5pm; free). It lies opposite Cathedral Square and was built in 1471 by Bishop Andrew Muirhead to house the master of the hospice of St Nicholas, who looked after a complement of 12 old men.

The house was saved and restored in 1906, with financial aid and period furnishings supplied by Sir Wil-

Provand's Lordship, the oldest Glasgow house still standing and now a museum portraying medieval life in the city.

Gruesome Tales

If spirits haunt any part of Glasgow, it should be here. Men and women were hanged outside the Tolbooth, and alleged witches and miscreants scourged. The original building had spikes on the walls for the decapitated heads of felons. When the justiciary decamped to the river end of the Saltmarket and the council moved west, the main part of the Tolbooth was lost; only the steeple and its winding stone staircase remain.

The Tolbooth has a long and gruesome history.

liam Burrell (see page 90) in 1927; it is now run by Glasgow Museums. Behind it lies a **Physic Garden**, in tribute to St Nicholas. The sound of the traffic gives way to medieval calm here, among the herb plantings and knot gardens. Behind the wall, towards the Strathclyde campus, is a small but ambitious orchard, where students convene under the spring blossom and try to ignore the M8 just up the road.

RELIGION AND MEDICINE

Back across the High Street – traffic is always bad here – is the **St Mungo Museum of Religious Life and Art** 8 (tel: 0141-276 1625; www.glasgowlife.org.uk; Tue–Thu, Sat 10am–5pm, Fri and Sun 11am–5pm; free), which, before it was opened in 1993, caused some controversy over whether it was an architectural pastiche. The honey-coloured stone building stands on the site of the medieval Bishop's Castle and houses works of art from the main religions – Buddhist, Christian, Hindu, Jewish, Muslim and Sikh – as well as minor ones. Religious rites are explained alongside intriguing relics and there are gorgeous views from the top floor.

A restored room at Provand's Lordship depicts medieval living.

Inside the Gallery of Religious Art there are powerful images of religious figures and rites to explore, including an imposing figure of the Hindu god Shiva, Lord of the Dance, and the Mexican Day of the Dead skeleton, which celebrates the victory of life over death. Illuminating the poignant images are some truly stunning stained-glass windows showing Christian saints and prophets. The museum's pleasant coffee shop backs

Quirky Shops

Along this sweep of handsome red-brick tenements – between the pubs and fish-and-chip takeaways – there are dishevelled shopfronts aplenty. But tucked in among the intriguing and slightly unsettling array of shops – from beauty/massage parlours and hairdressers to religious missions and a butcher or two – lies **23enigma** (258 High Street; tel: 0141-553 1990), bubbling with spell books, talismans and crystals. It even offers alternative therapies including hypnosis and reiki.

Tarot cards are just some of the spooky wares on offer at 23enigma.

The St Mungo Museum of Religious Life and Art has won awards for its fascinating exhibits and attempts to promote inter-faith understanding.

onto an attractive Zen-style garden designed by Yasutaro Tanaka – another unexpected haven of peace in this busy street.

The cathedral precinct is fronted by a statue of the Scots missionary explorer David Livingstone (see page 107) and provides an excellent foreground for the massive bulk of the **Royal Infirmary** ❾, which was completed in 1915 and commemorates the 65-year reign of Queen Victoria, whose solemn presence looms above the entrance. The Royal, which has been operating since 1794, has made a proud contribution to world medicine: Lord Lister pioneered antiseptic surgery here in the 1860s; Sir William Macewen established his reputation in brain surgery and osteopathy here in the 1890s; and his matron Mrs Rebecca Strong introduced the world's first systematic training for nurses. In the early part of the 19th

Initiation display at the St Mungo Museum of Religious Life and Art.

Barony Chapel, in the crypt of Glasgow Cathedral, is so named because it was used by Barony parishioners for their worship.

century, its resources were considerably stretched as it sought to cope with epidemics of cholera, typhus and dysentery. Today, it has one of the busiest casualty departments in Europe, coping with Glasgow's still prevalent weekend bouts of random and inventive violence.

GLASGOW CATHEDRAL

At the east end of the precinct lies **Glasgow Cathedral** ⑩ (tel: 0141-552 8198; www.glasgowcathedral.org; Apr–Sept Mon–Sat 9.30am–5.30pm, Sun 1–5pm, Oct–Mar Mon–Sat 9.30am–4.30pm, Sun 1–4.30pm). The tides of history have washed over this important ecclesiastical site since Glasgow's early days. It was founded in 1136 on the site of St Mungo's Church and has always been a focus for Christian learning and culture in Scotland. It has stood through the supremacy of the bishops, the War of Independence and the upheaval of the Reformation, and began to take the shape that we see today around the middle of the 14th century. Its blackened stone illustrates the colouring of many Glasgow buildings before stone-cleaning became widespread. Attempts have been made to clean it

Glasgow Cathedral is the best-preserved medieval church in Scotland.

The cathedral is known for its magnificent stained-glass windows.

up, but it was felt that it would cause too much damage.

The visitors' entrance is flanked by a memorial to the Hutcheson brothers and George Baillie, who 'divested himself of his fortune to endow institutions devoted to the intellectual culture of the operative classes'. The grounds are surrounded by gravestones. Blue-robed custodians belonging to the Society of Friends of Glasgow Cathedral give fascinating impromptu tours.

Music enthusiasts and anyone interested in the labyrinthine history of this colossal building will be keen to find out about the latest recitals and lectures held in the cathedral. Completing the warm welcome given to visitors and incredible resources available to the curious, there is the Congregations' Library, which is situated in the Cathedral Hall in the basement of the nearby St Mungo Museum (see page 18). It is open on Wednesday afternoons from 2pm to 4pm.

St Mungo

Legend has it that a century after St Ninian dedicated a Christian burial ground at Cathures (later Glasgow), Kentigern – popularly known as Mungo – arrived. Kentigern hailed from Culross in Fife (Glaswegians may be taken aback to learn that their patron saint was in fact a Fifer), where he was trained as a priest by St Serf. He accompanied the corpse of a holy man, Fergus – carried on a cart by two oxen – to the St Ninian's burial ground in Cathures, where Fergus was buried.

Architectural features

The main structure is a rectangle with a cross surmounted by a tower and steeple. A lower church opens up underneath the choir. Damaged by fire, the original cathedral building was succeeded by a larger one, which was consecrated in 1197. Major 13th-century rebuilding by William de Bondinton (1233–58) can be seen in the Quire and the Lower Church. Check out the doorways of the sac-

Images of St Mungo, Glasgow's patron saint, adorn the city.

risty (Upper Chapterhouse) and of the Lower Chapterhouse; these date from the mid-13th century. Extensive work enlarged the nave in the 14th century – for a closer look at these developments seek out the southwest door and the entrance to the Blacader Aisle, where the body of Fergus is said to have been buried by St Mungo (see page 21).

Other intriguing architectural and social developments occurred after the Reformation to allow three different congregations to worship in different spaces, reflecting rank and class divisions. From 1595, the Barony Parishioners worshipped in the lower church (crypt), while from 1648 the High Kirk congregation worshipped in the choir itself, and the nave was used by worshippers from the eastern part of the city. Ask one of the robed custodians for interesting tidbits from this period.

NECROPOLIS

At the south side of the Cathedral is a bridge that spans Wishart Street and leads to the **Necropolis** ⓫ (7am–dusk; free) an impressive ornamental garden cemetery modelled on Père-Lachaise in Paris. It is full of crumbling temples and monuments, many of which are in a sorry state of repair, which only adds to the chilling atmosphere, especially on dreich (dismal, gloomy) days.

In 1831, John Strang, Chamberlain at the Merchants' House, wrote *Necropolis Glasguensis* ('Thoughts on Death and Moral Stimulus'), which included an outline of city plans for the hilly site that had been previous-

Views From the Tombs

The splendid views from the hill housing the Necropolis not only give some idea of the imposing grandeur of the Cathedral in medieval times, but also stretch as far as Ben Lomond to the northwest and the Cathkin Braes to the south. Roe deer can be seen roaming between the monument obelisks and haughty headstones. The combination of wildlife and monumental Victorian display and decay – with a skyline backdrop of lines of high-rise flats and churches – is strangely spine-tingling.

Glasgow Cathedral seen from the Necropolis.

Memorials in the Victorian Necropolis.

ly known as Fir Park, which he considered to appear 'admirably adapted for a Pere la Chaise, which would harmonise beautifully with the adjacent scenery, and constitute a solemn and appropriate appendage to the venerable structure (the Cathedral) in front of which, while it will afford a much wanted accommodation to the higher classes, would at the same time convert an unproductive property into a general and lucrative source of profit, to a charitable institution'. It was to be 'respectful to the dead, safe and sanitary to the living, dedicated to the Genius of Memory and to extend religious and moral feeling'.

Chic fashion on the High Street.

Architect David Hamilton, Stuart Murray, Curator of the Botanic Gardens, and James Clelland, Superintendent of Public Works, produced a feasibility study for forming the Glasgow Necropolis, and in 1828 the committee of Directors of Lands and Quarries agreed to the proposal. Then in 1831, a competition for converting the Fir Park into a cemetery was launched, with five prizes of £10–50 up for grabs. As the burial ground was intended to be interdenominational, the first burial in 1832 was fittingly that of a Jew, Joseph Levi, a jeweller. Extensions into quarry ground in the 1860s and 1870s give us the present-day dimensions of 37 acres (15 hectares).

A walk around the graves

Some 50,000 burials have taken place at the Necropolis and most of the 3,500 tombs are about 14ft (4m)

Situated on a hill, the Necropolis offers wonderful views.

deep, with solid stone walls and brick partitions. Some of the Necropolis tombs on the top of the hill were blasted out of the rock face. Many of the monuments were designed by major architects and sculptors, including Alexander 'Greek' Thomson, Charles Rennie Mackintosh and J.T. Rochead, which makes a walk around the sprawling site a fascinating insight into both Victorian and Edwardian styles and tastes. The administration and maintenance of2 the Necropolis was handed from Merchants' House to Glasgow City Council in 1966.

A stone angel adorns a grave in the Necropolis.

The Necropolis's grand bridge was built by the Merchants' House of Glasgow to 'afford a proper entrance to the new cemetery combining convenient access to the grounds' and views of 'the venerable Cathedral and surrounding scenery'. Paths lead in circles round the hill past gloomy, ivy-clad, marble-pillared tombs and sombre obelisks. The Victorians took themselves as seriously in death as in life. The crowning monument on the summit is to John Knox, the austere father of the Reformation in Scotland, which 'produced a revolution in the sentiments of mankind'. Knox still keeps a suspicious eye on the city below. The Friends of Glasgow Necropolis (www.glasgownecropolis.org) is a superb organisation which runs tours of the site and various cultural events.

BACK TO GLASGOW CROSS

Leaving the cemetery in Wishart Street, this tour continues past the huge steel tanks of the **Tennent Caledonian Brewery**, which supplies a commodity as welcome to many Glaswegians as Loch Katrine's water. At the foot of the street the modern flats and high-rise blocks on the right stand on the site of the Drygate, one of the original streets of old Glasgow.

Turning right into Duke Street, past the former Alexander's School, now a business centre (adorned with busts of the heads of Shakespeare and other luminaries), the road follows along the wall of the old College Goods Yard.

To return to Glasgow Cross, turn left at the traffic lights and head into the High Street.

One of the Necropolis's elaborate tombs.

Eating Out

Babbity Bowster
16–18 Blackfriars Street; tel: 0141-552 5055; www.babbitybowster.com; pub 11am–midnight, restaurant dinner only Tue–Sat. Housed in a handsome Adam brothers-designed building, this popular hangout has the Schottische restaurant upstairs, serving hearty portions of Scottish classic dishes with a Gallic twist. The homely pub serves decent ales and malts to a live folk music soundtrack. This place is popular with a diverse crowd. £

St Mungo Museum Café
St Mungo Museum of Religious Life and Art; Tue–Thu, Sat 10am–4.30pm, Fri and Sun 11am–4.30pm. This museum café serves predominantly simple, honest British grub, as well as some pasta dishes, heaped salads and good-value soup of the day. There is also an attractive garden where you can enjoy your meal in good weather. £

Babbity Bowster.

The Barras, one of the biggest markets in Europe.

Tour 2

The Barras to Saltmarket

This short 2-mile (3.2km) walk takes in the banter and bargains of the Barras, Glasgow Green's delights and a short stroll south to the Clyde

If the High Street walk (see page 14) uncovers layers of Glasgow's history, this tour, which takes in the lively Barras, is where the city's working-class past meets modern struggles and endeavours. This walk is a real eye-opener and is bound to deliver some memorable, oddball stories, encounters and scenes.

Although at first glance this busy marketplace is tatty and run-down, the area is full of life and colour, and bargain-hunters flock to it from all over the city and beyond. Down towards the Clyde and over the bridge there are old and new popular Glaswegian institutions – including the People's Palace museum and the handsome Winter Gardens at Glasgow Green – as well as the Citizens Theatre and Central Mosque. Round the corner from historic folk music pubs there are notorious locations etched on the Glaswegian psyche, including Nelson's Pillar, sight of many a public hanging.

Highlights

- The Saracen's Head
- Exploring the Barras
- The People's Palace
- Glasgow Green
- Doulton Fountain
- St Andrew's Parish Church
- Central Mosque
- Citizens Theatre
- Clyde Walkway
- Saltmarket

Along the Clyde Walkway.

Saturday and Sunday are the best days to undertake this tour, as the majority of shops around the Saltmarket are open then.

ALONG GALLOWGATE

Starting the walk from the **Mercat Cross** (see page 14), head east up the **Gallowgate**, which is generally accepted to have the macabre meaning its name implies. However, the late historian George Eyre-Todd suggested that it meant the *gait*, or way to, the *gia lia*, or sacred stone of Celtic times, which would make it one of the oldest roads in Scotland. Social raconteur Jack House recalls days in the 1930s when the street housed 60 pubs and he 'never ventured there without an occasional *frisson* disturbing me'.

The road leads under a bridge, passing a row of discount shops, as well as Moir Street and Charlotte Street, after which you reach Glasgow's oldest chippie (1884) at Little Dovehill and then Great Dovehill on the left. According to legend, this is where St Mungo was preaching to his flock when someone at the back complained that he could not see him, whereupon he commanded the adjoining ground to rise up in the air.

A little further along, you will come to **The Saracen's Head** ❶ (Sat 11am–11pm, Sun 12.30–11pm), or 'The Sarry Heid', a pub whose glory days are most definitely behind it. It lays claim to being the first real hotel in Glasgow, built in 1755 from the ruins of the old bishop's castle, and takes its name from a 12th-century

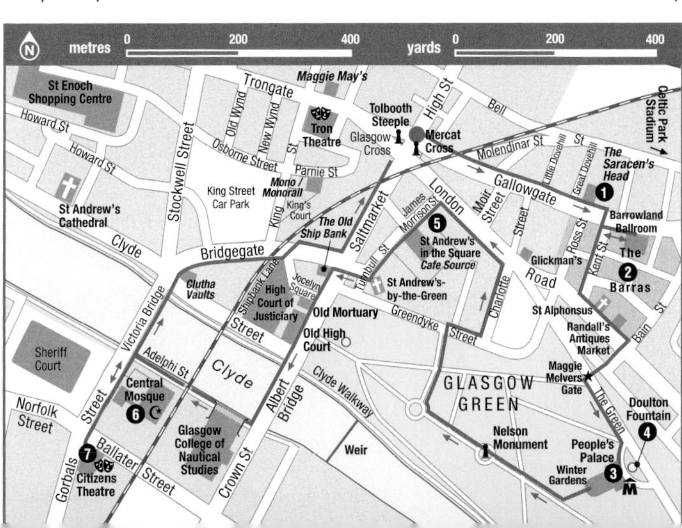

The Barras market takes its name from the Glaswegian dialect for 'barrow'; in the market's early years, the traders sold their goods from handcarts.

inn in London frequented by Richard the Lionheart. The first mail coach from London arrived here in 1788, and it was a haunt of Scotland's judges as they progressed round the western circuit from Edinburgh.

THE BARRAS

Crossing the road to Kent Street, **The Barras** ❷ (http://theglasgowbarras.com; Sat–Sun 9.30am–4.30pm) originated as a street market consisting of hand-barrows hired out by the McIver family to traders too poor to have their own. The covered market came into being in 1926 and, after a spell in the doldrums in the 1970s and 1980s, it has been revitalised and is now said to be one of the biggest markets in Europe.

Second-hand furniture and clothes predominate, although in keeping with the times, DVDs, computer games and CDs, whose legality is continu-

Sarry Heid's Inn

The old inn has been visited by an impressive list of patrons, including Robert Burns, John Wesley, James Boswell, William Wordsworth and Adam Smith, who was allegedly ejected after a swearing match with Dr Samuel Johnson. It houses the 1760 Saracen's Head punchbowl and the skull of Maggie (the last witch to be burned at the stake), which the title deeds demand is to be passed to the People's Palace if the pub is ever demolished.

The Sarry Heid's inn displays a range of quirky artefacts.

The Barrowland Ballroom is a popular venue with a variety of local and high-profile international acts, who praise the acoustics and atmosphere.

ally challenged by trading standards officers, now feature. Slightly further along the Gallowgate from the Kent Street entrance is the **Barrowland Ballroom**, a dance hall that was the focus of the 1960s Bible John murders – when three women were killed by a man with a penchant for quoting Old Testament texts to his victims – but is now one of Glasgow's largest live music venues, staging gigs by local bands and international stars, including one of Dumbarton's finest sons, David Byrne.

In case you are wondering about the green-and-white-striped men often seen staggering along the Gallowgate, chanting musical ditties, these are fans of Celtic Football Club, popularly know as 'Hoops'. Among the many bars to and from **Celtic Park Stadium**, a 15-minute walk east of the Barras, was the legendary Baird's Bar, next door to the Barrowland Ballroom. The Baird was well known as a Hoops' haunt and pre-gig watering hole, but the authorities finally called time on it in 2013, following repeated violent clashes. Steeped in decades of football history, it was here that former player and manager Kenny Dalglish, MBE famously held a press conference in 2000.

Kent Street leads through to London Road, and, turning left, you'll see St Alphonsus Church. Next door is **Randall's Antiques Market** (Sat–Sun 9am–5pm), which has a café attached. Proceed down Bain Street, through the Maggie McIvers Gate, and into **Glasgow Green**. Through the trees you will see the exotic coloured-brick frontage of the old Templeton's carpet factory, an enthusiastic copy of the Doge's Palace in Venice, designed by William Leiper in 1889. The factory is now a business centre.

Shopping for fruit and veg at the Barras; a farmers' market is also held here on the last Saturday of the month.

PEOPLE'S PALACE

Turn left for the **People's Palace** ❸ (tel: 0141-276 0788; www.glasgowlife.org.uk; Tue–Thu and Sat 10am–5pm, Fri and Sun 11am–5pm; free), a museum presiding over one of the tree-lined avenues of Glasgow Green and a favourite with Glaswegians. It was built in 1898 as a cultural centre for workers, who were living in some of the most abject conditions of the Industrial age. Lord Rosebery outlined the purpose of the grandiose civic project: 'A palace of pleasure and imagination around which the people may place their affections and which may give them a home on which their memory may rest'. He then declared the building as 'Open to the people for ever and ever'.

Originally, the ground floor provided space for reading and recreation, with a museum on the first floor, and a picture gallery on the top floor. Since the 1940s it has concentrated on the history and the way of life of the working class as well as kings and cardinals. Exhibits range from a ring that belonged to Mary, Queen of Scots to comedian Billy Connolly's 'banana boots'. The red-sandstone building, with its domed roof and pillared frontage, was completely refurbished for its centenary in 1998 and now uses the latest computer technology and film to tell its story.

The Winter Gardens, where you can wander among exotic plants.

Display at the People's Palace.

Strolling on Glasgow Green.

On the top floor is a powerful series of paintings by artist and Glasgow School of Art graduate Ken Currie, who was commissioned to mark the 1987 bicentenary of the massacre of Glasgow's Calton weavers, Scotland's first trade union martyrs. The series of eight paintings adorns the splendid dome: the cycle begins in 1787 and ends with a vision of the future. It traces the development of the Scottish labour movement through Currie's powerful imagery. **The Winter Gardens** (daily 10am–5pm), a huge conservatory housing tropical palms and ferns, butts onto the back of the Palace. After a serious fire in 1998, it has now reopened and houses a café-cum-bar.

GLASGOW GREEN

In 1450 Bishop Turnbull gave the common lands of **Glasgow Green** to the people of the city, although its previously rural vista is now bounded by the high-rise flats of the Gorbals, across the river. Bonnie Prince Charlie mustered his armies here, and the Glasgow Fair, instituted in 1190, is still celebrated in the park in the last fortnight of July. Turning right past the palace, a 144ft (44m) needle erected to commemorate Lord Nelson dominates the western end.

In front of the People's Palace, the magnificent red-terracotta **Doulton Fountain** ❹, gifted by the Victorian china manufacturer to commemorate Queen Victoria's Golden Jubilee of 1887, has been restored with investment from the National Lottery Fund. Its five-tier, 46ft (14m) -high and 70ft (21m) -wide display of imperial pride makes it the largest terracotta fountain in the world and a mesmerising insight into Glasgow's prominent place in the British Empire. It was first unveiled at the Empire Exhibition held at Kelvingrove Park in 1888 and then moved to Glas-

Banana Boots

These outrageous boots became Scottish star Billy Connolly's trademark. Designed by Glaswegian Edmund Smith, on completion of the first banana he indicated that the second would not be identical – and so the second banana was given 'designer status' by adding the famous Fyffes label. The boots made their first appearance on stage in Aberdeen in August 1975.

The splendid People's Palace and Doulton Fountain on Glasgow Green.

Independent Shopping

It may have the Barras and some scruffy old markets, but this area is not renowned for its upmarket shopping. However, there are a few excellent independent shops and specialist outlets that are well worth seeking out. **Monorail** (12 Kings Court, King Street; tel: 0141-552 9458; Mon–Sat 11am–7pm, Sun noon–7pm) is run by Pastels front man Stephen Pastel, and is a must for musos and vinyl addicts. They have a great vegan-friendly café and a space for cultural events and cinema screenings. Just north of Monorail is Glasgow's best comic shop, **A1 Comics** (35 Parnie Street; tel: 0141-552 6692; daily 10am–6pm, Sun noon–5pm), which has some fine toys for kids and objects for geeky adults alongside piles of Marvel and DC editions. A fund for shop owners on Saltmarket and St Andrew's Street has been put in place to assist the upkeep of premises. It is hoped that this move will enhance the appeal of Saltmarket and further increase the number of independent shops.

gow Green in 1890. Walk around it to get a closer look at extravagant figurative groups representing Australia, Canada, India and South Africa. Seek out national flora and fauna (Australian sheep, Canadian beaver and South Africa's ostrich), alongside military and naval figures including a kilted highlander. Completing the array of dizzying decorations are gargoyles, coats of arms, lion masks and young girls pouring water over the figures below. Topping the whole Imperial enterprise is a lifelike statue of Queen Victoria.

The music shop Monorail is heaven for vinyl lovers.

Nelson's Pillar (1806) was the first civic monument in Britain to commemorate the Admiral's victories.

ST ANDREW'S IN THE SQUARE

Returning north to London Road, along Charlotte Street, is Glickman's fabulous confectionery shop (est. 1903), paradise for anyone with a sweet tooth. The tour continues towards Glasgow Cross and left into James Morrison Street and St Andrew's Square, which is home to **St Andrew's Parish Church** ❺ (now known as **St Andrew's in the Square**), the oldest church in the city after the Cathedral. It was modelled on St Martin-in-the-Fields in London, and its massive pillars and stone ornamentation illustrate the grand tastes of the 18th-century Tobacco Lords. It now stages musical and other cultural events, and houses the excellent Café Source (see page 37).

The south side of the square passes the district courts, where minor offenders are daily chastised, and, turning left and then right into Steel Street, the route leads to the Saltmarket. The pub on the facing corner, **The Old Ship Bank**, recalls the first Glasgow bank, set up in 1750 to meet the needs of the influential and rising merchant class. Going left down the Saltmarket, the new **High Court of Justiciary** extension is tucked into Jocelyn Square behind the old Mortuary. Further along is the old High Court, with its forbidding grey-pillared portico, which has seen the black cap donned for a procession of murderers. It fronted onto Jail Square, where the guilty were hanged before cheering crowds in the shadow of Nelson's Pillar, giving rise to the maternal Glaswegian warning to recalcitrant children: 'You'll die facing the monument.'

TOWARDS AND OVER THE CLYDE

Saltmarket runs down onto the **Albert Bridge**, or Hutchesontown Bridge, a cast-iron structure built in

St Andrew's in the Square has been restored to its 18th-century glory.

Inside the Citizens Theatre.

1871 on enormous granite piers on the site of a crossing first created in 1794. Just upstream is the weir, which marks the tidal limit of the river and controls its natural vagaries. Over the bridge, appropriately at the river's junction with the sea, is what was the **Glasgow College of Nautical Studies**, which merged with the City of Glasgow College in 2010.

Turning right onto the south bank of the river at the start of the college, a tree-lined walkway leads to the peaceful colonnaded grounds of the **Central Mosque** ❻ (tel: 0141-429 3132; www.centralmosque.co.uk; daily for prayers; guided tours by arrangement), which in 1984 became the first purpose-built mosque in Scotland and is now one of the largest in Europe. Its green, multi-faceted dome and soaring minaret combine Islamic architecture with traditional Scottish sandstone. It provides the facilities of worship for 2,000 Muslims, a community whose numbers have increased dramatically in recent deacdes and who now play an integral part in city life.

The forbidding black-and-grey-marbled building on the other side of Gorbals Street is the **Sheriff Court**, where solicitors gather to ply an ancient trade. It moved here when the old, smaller, city-centre court became unable to cope with the numbers that make it the busiest court in Europe.

Further south down Gorbals Street, across the junction with Ballater Street, is the **Citizens Theatre** ❼ (tel: 0141-429 0022; www.

The Albert Bridge.

Clyde Walkway

This 40-mile (64km) -long path has been developed to link Glasgow with the Falls of Clyde at Lanark. Cyclists and walkers will particularly enjoy the Glasgow section between Victoria Bridge and the SECC, which passes the PS *Waverley* Terminal – home of the world's last sea-going paddle steamer – and the colossal 176ft (54m) -high Finnieston Crane, which once raised railway locomotives. There are a number of other long-distance paths that link up with the Clyde Walkway, including the Kelvin Walkway, the West Highland Way and paths to Edinburgh, Greenock and Irvine.

See ongoing riverside development from the Clyde Walkway.

citz.co.uk), a cornerstone of Glasgow's artistic life and a major contributor to its ambition to be considered as a European city. The Citizen's Company was established in 1943 amid a row of Gorbals tenements, in a grand Victorian building originally called His Majesty's Theatre, which had been opened in 1878. Scottish playwright James Bridie drove the project as part of a plan to establish a Scottish national theatre. It drifted from drama into crisis until the arrival in 1969 of director Giles Havergal and his flamboyant designer Philip Prowse. Their ground-breaking pro-

The Central Mosque.

Gothic-spired St Andrew's Cathedral is now dwarfed by the modern riverside buildings.

ductions – sometimes shocking and disturbing – attracted headlines and interest far beyond Glasgow and continue to fill the hall. The theatre houses a main auditorium and two small studio theatres which offer cutting-edge works.

HEADING BACK NORTH OF THE CLYDE

Returning along Gorbals Street, the road comes to **Victoria Bridge**, where the city's first river crossing, a wooden structure commissioned by Bishop Rae in 1350, stood for 450 years. The present bridge is faced with Dublin granite and affords excellent views down river past the Carlton Place Suspension Bridge to the Jamaica Street and Central Station bridges. The Gothic-spired building on the north bank is **St Andrew's Cathedral** (www.cathedralg1.org; Mon–Fri 7.30am–5.45pm, Sat 7.30am–6.15pm, Sun 9am–6.15pm), the main Roman Catholic church, which is reflected in the modern glass-walled diocesan headquarters next door. The cathedral reopened in 2011 after substantial renovation and includes a new baptismal font and a new artwork of St Andrew and the city's patron saint St Mungo. The glass pyramids rising above the rooftops behind it are the canopies of the St Enoch shopping centre.

Across the bridge, on the north bank, is a Glasgow music institution, Clutha Vaults. Sadly, this bar is now

Coffee and music at Monorail.

better known for a helicopter crash in 2013 that took 10 lives. The area of the roof that the helicopter plunged into has been repaired, but parts of the pub have been left untouched. At a poignant ceremony in July 2015, First Minister Nicola Sturgeon, joined by relatives and survivors, reopened its doors once again. Intentions are to create a lasting memorial for the victims' families.

A NEW CULTURAL QUARTER

Veering right into the Bridgegate, or Briggait, one of Glasgow's oldest streets, the three-tiered spire of the old fish market catches your eye. Built in 1873, the building is on the cusp of becoming a new creative space. Under the railway bridge, on waste ground between St Margaret's Place and the new High Court buildings, is where **Paddy's Market** was held until May 2009. The defunct market had its origins, as the name suggests, in the floods of refugees from the Irish potato famine. The area is set to be transformed into a new cultural quarter to link up with the exciting new artsy venues and bars on the Trongate and Merchant City (see page 40). Some residents have not taken kindly to gentrifying the area, but most see the benefit of transforming it into a bustling centre of arts and enterprise.

Turning left at the end of the Briggait, the **Saltmarket** – so named because the original market for salt for curing river salmon was here – curves back up to the High Street past restored tenements and shops.

Eating Out

Café Source
1 St Andrew's Square; tel: 0141-548 6020; http://cafesource.co.uk; daily lunch and dinner.
Locally sourced ingredients go into the hearty fare served in the basement of St Andrew's in the Square. £

Maggie's Kitchen
60 Trongate; tel: 0141-548 1350; http://maggiemays.info; daily lunch and dinner.
Hidden in the back of the busy Maggie May's bar on the Trongate, this intimate place concentrates on traditional Scots fare with some imaginative additions. Standouts include Maggie's famous pie of the day, and sticky toffee pudding. £

Mono
12 King's Court, King Street; tel: 0141-553 2400; www.monocafebar.com; bar Sun–Thu 11am–11pm, Fri–Sat until 1am; kitchen daily noon–9pm.
A popular music and arts venue with a great record shop, Mono also squeezes in a café with a vegan menu. Top dishes include the falafel sharing platter served with tzatziki, flatbread and hummous, and the Mono veggie burger. £

Sandstone & Steel

Roads, slum clearances, high-rise schemes and recession may have savaged the city in the past, but Glasgow's innovative spirit is reinvigorating the urban landscape

SOLID SANDSTONE SPIRIT

In Glasgow's city centre, grand drama and extravagance in sculpted stone predominates.

From the weathered 13th-century remnants found in the vicinity of Glasgow Cathedral and the 17th-century mercantile optimism around the Trongate, to the grandeur of the mansions of the Tobacco Lords in the Merchant City in the 18th century and the robust flowering of the Victorians in the British Empire's heyday, Glasgow developed into a city carved painstakingly from sandstone.

Although Charles Rennie Mackintosh (see page 94) and Alexander 'Greek' Thomson are foremost in the current view of Glasgow's architectural heritage, others such as William Young – who created the City Chambers as a monument to civic pride in 1888 – J.T. Rochead, J.J. Burnet and Charles Wilson all contributed mightily. Rochead's work in St Vincent Street sets the tone for the commercial centre, and his Grosvenor Hotel is a true Venetian marvel, Burnet's former TSB banking hall on the corner of Ingram Street and Glassford Street outshines the bigger surroundings, while Wilson created an

Tradeston Bridge in Atlantic Quay, nicknamed 'squiggly' because of its S-shaped design.

Italianate skyscape in the Park Circus area which is unequalled in Britain.

Huge enterprises such as Robert Anderson's Central Hotel and the Edwardian mass of the Royal Technical College (now the University of Strathclyde) vie for attention amongst small-scale confections including James Miller's miniature version of France's Azay-le-Rideau in the centre of St Enoch Square.

GLASS, STEEL AND THE FUTURE

Modern architecture in Glasgow is following a bold tradition. Atlantic Quay on the Clyde has waterfront grandeur, as does the Clyde Auditorium (dubbed the Armadillo for its distinctive shape) by Sir Norman Foster and its neighbour the SSE Hydro. The Glasgow Science Centre complex has titanium curves and a soaring viewing tower, called the Titan. The open-plan interior of the new BBC Scotland building on Pacific Quay is equally bold; so, too, is the Clyde Arc Bridge (known locally as the Squinty Bridge).

Other visionary projects include the striking Riverside Museum, designed by star architect Zaha Hadid, with its wave-like 'pleated' aluminium shapes, and the Glasgow School of Art addition, opposite Mackintosh's architectural masterpiece, completed in 2014. In September 2009, Steven Holl Architects' (New York) light-filled design won a high-profile competition to build the GSA's new teaching and research centre.

Other recent projects have imaginatively adapted some of Glasgow's old sandstone architecture. To the innovative renovations at the Italian Centre, Tron Theatre and Princes Square can be added Trongate 103, a cutting-edge arts hub hewn out of an Edwardian warehouse. It's all part of Glasgow City Council's plan to regenerate this part of the Merchant City down to the River Clyde, and in doing so create an enlarged cultural quarter.

A great way to absorb Glasgow's exciting architecture is on a guided tour. For information about Glasgow Architectural Walking Tours, including a visit to the GSA, check out www.glasgowarchitecture.co.uk.

Café life in the Italian Centre in John Street.

Tour 3

Merchant City

From Trongate's vibrant arts centres, this half-day ¾-mile (1.2km) walk delves into the heart of the Merchant City's cool hangouts, conversions and enterprising institutions

The Merchant City fell into decline during the 1980s recession, leaving huge warehouses abandoned and businesses boarded up. Ambitious developments and stylish conversions, added to visionary arts projects such as the Tron Theatre and Trongate 103, have brought the area back to life. Expect an earthy mix of arty creativity and working-class wit.

While other cities have wrestled with inner-city problems, Glasgow perversely had an outer-city problem. Huge schemes – Drumchapel, Easterhouse, Castlemilk and Pollok, which were created after World War II to facilitate slum clearance – stand guard at each corner of the boundaries. In the late 1970s and early 1980s, Glasgow was tagged Doughnut City – plenty round the outside and nothing in the middle. The Merchant City was Glasgow's attempt to bring life back to the central warehouse district. The square-mile area is now home to a core of

Highlights

- Tron Theatre
- Trongate 103
- Old Fruitmarket
- Ramshorn Kirk and Cemetery
- City Halls
- Old Glasgow Sheriff Court
- Hutchesons' Hall
- Italian Centre
- Trades Hall

The stylish Trongate 103.

young professionals and arty types. The blend of old and new architecture creates an exciting fusion that is echoed in the many restaurants serving up innovative cross-cultural food. Alongside exciting arts developments including the Tron Theatre and Trongate 103 there's a wealth of pubs, clubs and independent shops. Keep your eyes peeled on partnership plans with Glasgow City Council for the Merchant City's next phase of arts-led regeneration, which is heading south of the Trongate, to create a cultural quarter down to the Clyde.

ALONG THE TRONGATE

Starting the route at the old heart of the city at **Mercat Cross** (see page 14), go west along the Trongate. The tenements along each side date from the middle and end of the 19th century, and their rich facades funnel the street along to an almost Central European steeple, with a base that forms an open arch across the busy pavement. This is **Tron-St Mary's**, a former church. Like the street, it is named after the weighing machine, or tron, introduced by the Bishop of Glasgow in 1491 to weigh and tax goods coming into the city. The church has been operating as the **Tron Theatre** ❶ (tel: 0141-552 4267; www.tron.co.uk) since 1982, first as a club, and since 1990 as a full public venue. The Tron Theatre features a programme of both contemporary and traditional Scottish drama, and its restaurant – which offers cracking lunchtime and pre-theatre menus – is a popular meeting place.

Continuing westwards along the Trongate you come to the impressive **Trongate 103** ❷ (tel: 0141-276 8380; Tue–Sat 10am–5pm, Sun noon–5pm), a massive Edwardian warehouse converted into an exciting arts centre, which opened in 2009. Beyond the cavernous contemporary atrium – imaginatively hewn out of the old handsome red-sandstone warehouse – are five floors of print studios, retail shops and galleries, where artists and the public can mingle and exchange ideas.

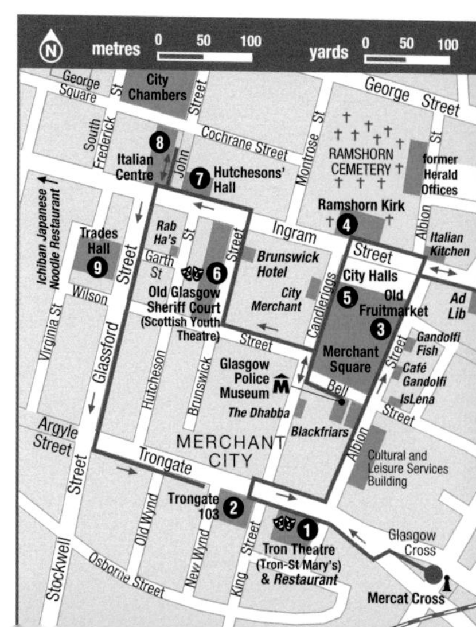

Exploring the Trongate, the old centre of the city.

UP ALBION STREET AND THE OLD FRUITMARKET

Crossing Trongate, head back eastwards then up Albion Street, past a magnificent red-sandstone bas-relief on the Cultural and Leisure Services building on the right, to the junction with Bell Street. This intersection has more pubs than the rest of both long streets put together. On the left, **Blackfriars** is large and lively, with a basement that hosts live music nights; **Café Gandolfi**, on the right, was one of the original Merchant City restaurants and contains the fantastical wood furniture of Tim Stead. **Gandolfi Fish**, an excellent seafood haunt, is just a few doors along. There are lots of lively pubs and restaurants that occupy various old buildings, including the **Old Fruitmarket** ❸, linked to Merchant Square.

The fruit market moved here from its former congested home in 1969 and now nestles, with the fish market, beside the M8 at Blochairn. The south end housed a successful general market for many years before closing to accommodate the new pubs. The north end, however, lay closed for years, until enthusiasts from the performing arts section of the council realised that its cobbled streets and balconied offices, which used to ring to the iron wheels of carts and the shouts of traders, would make an ideal, New

Gandolfi Fish.

The Old Fruitmarket packs lots of period charm under its vaulted roof.

Orleans-style venue for the annual **Glasgow Jazz Festival**. The extensively refurbished Old Fruitmarket is a much-loved performance space and hosts regular events and parties.

Next to the Old Fruitmarket, Glasgow-based artist Sam Bates was commissioned by Glasgow City Council to do a series of pieces promoting the 2014 Commonwealth Games. This striking street art depicts the four seasons in a picturesque Scottish country scene, featuring an array of animals.

Trongate 103 gallery.

Art @ Trongate 103

Resident organisations at Trongate 103 include the Russian Cultural Centre and Café Cosachock, Glasgow Print Studio, Street Level Photoworks, Transmission Gallery, Glasgow Project Room and Project Ability. Don't miss a journey into the darkly magic world of wonders and nuances of the Sharmanka (Russian for hurdy gurdy) Kinetic Theatre. This atmospheric space chimes with the workings of Edward Bersudsky and Tatyana Jakovskaya's fantastical inventions: a mesmerising, gently unfolding whirl of mechanical finds, *objets trouvés* and sculptural inventions, accompanied by crackly old Eastern European music.

Ramshorn Cemetery is the final resting place of some illustrious figures.

The building above the excellent **Italian Kitchen** pizzeria and café (www.italian-kitchen.co.uk), where Albion Street crosses Ingram Street, housed the original Mitchell Library collection on two floors in 1877. Stephen Mitchell came from a tobacco family and left a huge estate to provide books 'on all subjects not immoral' for the edification of the city's working classes. His initiative was the impetus for the public library service; today, the Mitchell Library (see page 63) is the largest public reference library in Europe.

On the opposite corner, Greenwich Village-style loft apartments are situated in a former Strathclyde University building. Further up Albion Street, the four-storey black-glass office formerly housed ***The Herald*** newspaper, which prides itself on being the world's oldest English-language daily. The newspaper has moved to offices in the city centre and the old offices have been turned into flats.

INGRAM STREET AND THE RAMSHORN

Looking right along Ingram Street, the **Ad Lib** bar/diner (tel: 0141-552 5736) on the right-hand side is housed in a red-sandstone building with a splendid coat of arms over the entrance. This was the Central Fire Station, built in 1899, and the home of Wallace the Fire Dog, the mascot who faithfully escorted the engines on their dangerous missions. The engine room used to contain a memorial to the 19 firemen who died in the Cheapside Street whisky bond blaze in 1960, an event that still scars the memory of many families in the city.

As you turn left along Ingram Street, the **Ramshorn Kirk** ❹ looms out of a grove of unlikely urban elms. The Gothic church with its square clock tower is properly known as St David's

Gothic Ramshorn Kirk.

Retail Therapy

Merchant City has swanky boutiques and speciality shops aplenty. Ingram Street is lined by elegant sandstone buildings harbouring exclusive designer labels, not least the ravishing former bank that is now home to **Jigsaw** (No. 177; tel: 0141-552 7639). Other labels nearby include **Ralph Lauren**, **Mulberry** and **Hugo Boss**. If it's jewellery you're after, head to **Brazen** (58 Albion Street; tel: 0141-552 4551), where you'll find unique pieces by independent designers. If your tummy is rumbling, go to **Top Tier Designer Cakes** (70 Bell Street; tel: 0141-552 2195) for a sugar fix of mouth-watering treats.

The Mulberry shop on Ingram Street.

(Ramshorn) and was built in 1824 on the Ramshorn estate. Thomas Rickman, a Birmingham architect, was chosen to design the present building upon the site of an 18th-century 'God Box'-style church. Its alluring design is based on a late 13th- and 14th-century Gothic design. Those tall and narrow, beautifully proportioned dimensions, soaring stained-glass windows, and substantial crypt show all the hallmarks of Gothic Revival Scots Style. It is built in handsome blond sandstone mined from a nearby quarry at Cowcaddens, and its tower – towards the front of the building – is 120ft (36m) high and houses a set of bells, which have never been rung.

The **Ramshorn Cemetery** is a verdant respite from street noise and a fascinating voice from the past. Many gravestones are so old as to be illegible, and some are still barred and spiked against the predations of grave robbers. Emile L'Angelier, arsenic victim of the infamous Madeleine Smith, is buried here, as is David Dale, philanthropic co-founder of New Lanark, and John 'Phosphorus' Anderson, the ebullient father of Strathclyde University. On the pavement outside, worn by thousands of careless feet, are the initials RF and AF, marking the resting place of the Foulis brothers, a pair of enterprising and painstaking printers who perfected the craft for Glasgow University in the 18th century. Robert Foulis was also instrumental in establishing an Academy of Arts some 14 years before the Royal Academy in London.

CITY HALLS AND CANDLERIGGS

The Ramshorn stands sentinel at the head of Candleriggs, a street that takes its name from the noisome candleworks that initially operated well away from the main population. This is the heart of the Merchant City, with coffee houses and fashionable bars on the right and the substantially refurbished **City Halls** ❺, where Dickens drew crowds for his read-

This red-sandstone building houses a stylish café.

ings and where every hue of political opinion has been heard, on the left. When the halls were built in 1841, they could accommodate an astonishing 3,500 people.

The traditional shoebox-style auditorium is still renowned today throughout the world for its incredible acoustics. It's a busy hub for musicians and is well worth checking out: the Glasgow Centre for Music inside is a friendly organisation based here, with lots of information about upcoming concerts and public workshops. The BBC Scottish Symphony Orchestra is also based here; in addition, the auditorium hosts performances by the Scottish Chamber Orchestra. For all the latest about City Halls performances and affiliated venues nearby (the Old Fruitmarket, Glasgow Royal Concert Hall) pop in, call 0141-353 8000 or check out www.glasgowconcerthalls.com.

Hutchesons' Hall has been at its present location on Ingram Street since 1806.

Further down on the left, the pavement outside the City Halls has some interesting marblework, created when the street cobbles were renewed, reflecting the area's age.

WILSON STREET

At the junction of Candleriggs and Bell Street, the **Glasgow Police Museum** (www.policemuseum.org.uk; Apr–Oct Mon–Sat 10am–4.30pm, Sun noon–4.30pm, Nov–Mar Tue and Sun, same hours; free) gives an insight into the history of Britain's first police force, as well as featuring exhibits on international policing.

Turning right from Candleriggs into Wilson Street, new flats mix with the imposing bulk of the old warehouse district and smart design shops nestle below. Continuing right into Brunswick Street, a sandstone Victorian building with huge Ionic columns occupies the entire block. This was the **Old Glasgow Sheriff Court ❻**, which opened in 1892 and closed in 1984, having witnessed nearly a century of unmitigated villainy. It once housed a whipping table (now in Strathclyde Police's Black Museum in Pitt Street) and was said to be haunted by a lady in white.

The building is currently being used as the home of the Scottish Youth Theatre and offers conference and exhibition space for hire.

Passing the **Brunswick Hotel** on the right, the flats at the corner of Brunswick Street and Ingram Street are a fine example of facade retention. The site was originally the warehouse premises of Campbell, Stewart & McDonald, and was one of the first in the Merchant City to tear out and replace the whole interior while keeping the architecturally important shell. The same thing is now happening with new district council buildings across the road.

HUTCHESONS' HALL

The white building on the opposite side of Ingram Street is **Hutchesons' Hall ❼**. Statues of George and Thomas Hutcheson, brothers from a land-owning family, peer down from niches in the Neoclassical front.

On his death in 1639, Thomas Hutcheson made provision for a hospital for 12 'poore decrippet men'. George

Scottish Youth Theatre

Established in 1976, the Scottish Youth Theatre (Old Sheriff Court, 105 Brunswick Street; tel: 0141-552 3988; www.scottishyouththeatre.org) organises an eclectic programme of classes and performances dedicated to young people of all ages, up to 25 years old. Productions are staged in the Brian Cox Studio (named after the Dundonian star of Hollywood blockbusters *Rob Roy, Braveheart* and *The Bourne Supremacy*) and theatres around the country.

Inside the light-filled Scottish Youth Theatre.

added more funds on his death two years later. The hospital was originally in the Trongate, and moved to its present location in 1806 to a design by David Hamilton, with further reconstruction work by John Baird in 1876. The interior is simply stunning. It was acquired in 1982 by the National Trust for Scotland (www.nts.org.uk), whose renovations over the years have been scrupulous and sympathetic. Following yet further restorations, the building reopened in June 2014 as a three-floor dining venue (www.hutchesonsglasgow.com), where its beautiful interior can be admired at leisure.

ITALIAN CENTRE AND TRADES HALL

Just past Hutchesons' Hall is the pedestrianised concourse of the **Italian Centre** ❽ in John Street. In this short stretch, on a sunny summer day, Glasgow can consider itself to be a European city. White-aproned waiters rush back and forth to tables of animated diners talking on their mobiles below the restaurants' canopies. A bronze of Mercury keeps an eye on the shoppers with their Armani and Versace bags, and the view up through the arches of the City Chambers (see page 51) is a symphony in stone. Shona Kinloch's humorous sculpture entitled *Thinking of Bella* and the Zen-calm slow flow of a water feature counterpoise the clamour for *Italian fashion* fripperies.

Italian Centre statuary.

Leaving the Italian Centre, you'll see a squat domed building on the corner of Glassford Street housing a retail outlet. The edifice was designed by John Burnet and is a splendid example of late Victorian confidence. Slightly further down on the same side is the **Trades Hall** ❾ (tel: 0141-552 2418; open to the public by arrangement, call for details), which, apart from the Cathedral, is the oldest building in the city that still fulfils its original function. It is the home of the 14 trades of Glasgow, which include hammermen, fleshers, bonnetmakers, weavers and barbers (who were the early surgeons). Their symbol – 14 arrows bound together – adorns the magnificent curving staircase that leads into the grand hall. The hall is lined with a magnificent mirrored silk frieze – the 3-D of its time – showing the trades about their business.

The Trades Hall is also the home of the Trades House, where business these days is mainly philanthropic – it dispenses more than £1 million a year in charity. It is worth a visit, especially for the benches carved by Belgian refugees in the entranceway, the Adam plasterwork and wood ceilings, and the kists, or chests, which are opened only once a year and contain a time capsule of trinkets dating back to 1604.

Return to Glasgow Cross by following Glassford Street south and turning left into Trongate.

The Trades Hall offers a fascinating look at the 14 traditional city trades.

Eating Out

Café Gandolfi
64 Albion Street; tel: 0141-552 6813; www.cafegandolfi.com; daily 8am–11.30pm.
A stylish, light-filled bar-restaurant with beautiful wood furniture serving simply prepared dishes such as smoked haddie with pea and onion mashed potatoes and a poached egg. Neighbouring Gandolfi Fish is its sleeker cousin. £

City Merchant
97–99 Candleriggs; tel: 0141-553 1577; www.citymerchant.co.uk; Mon–Sat lunch and dinner, Sun dinner only.
Quality modern Scottish cuisine specialising in meat and seafood. Try the superb Loch Etive oysters and mussels. ££

The Dhabba
44 Candleriggs; tel: 0141-553 1249; www.thedhabba.com; daily lunch and dinner.
Superb North Indian cooking; the speciality is dum pukht, curry cooked in a special dish that seals in the juices. Dishes such as tiger prawns from the clay tandoori oven are also recommended. ££

Ichiban Japanese Noodle Restaurant
50 Queen Street; tel: 0141-204 4200; www.ichiban.co.uk; Mon–Thu noon–10pm, Fri–Sat noon–11pm, Sun 1–10pm.
Minimalist, with steaming bowls of noodles served at long benches. £

IsLeña
51 Bell Street; tel 0141-552 3530; www.islenaglasgow.co.uk; daily breakfast, lunch and dinner.
Large windows and striking blue shades deliver an authentic Catalonian vibe. Good selection of small plates – try the beef carpaccio and chorizo picante. ££

Rab Ha's
83 Hutcheson Street, Merchant City; tel: 0141-572 0400; www.rabhas.com; Wed–Sat dinner only.
This basement restaurant offers international seafood and meat dishes. £

Tron Theatre Restaurant
63 Trongate; tel: 0141-552 8587; www.tron.co.uk; Sun–Mon lunch only, Tue–Sat lunch and dinner.
Serves no-nonsense British dishes using locally sourced ingredients. Great pre-theatre meal deals. £

Buchanan Street is always busy with shoppers.

Tour 4

City Centre

This 1-mile (1.6km) tour takes you from the sumptuous George Square and merchants' powerhouses to the shops of Buchanan Street, stopping to visit the Gallery of Modern Art

This half-day walk starts amid the bustle around Queen Street Station and the grand expanse of George Square, which contains the lavish City Chambers. Keep your wits about you amid the workaday melee as you will find your eyes are constantly drawn upwards to scan the wealth of mighty stonework built by Glasgow's old governmental and mercantile powerhouses.

Between visits to old bank building conversions and the experience of being swamped by the Buchanan Street shopping crowds, take a breather in the popular Gallery of Modern Art and enjoy the light-filled environs of one of the numerous swanky Princes Square top-floor eateries.

Highlights

- George Square
- City Chambers
- Gallery of Modern Art (GoMA)
- St George's Tron
- Stock Exchange Building
- Buchanan Street and Princes Square Shopping
- Merchants' House

QUEEN STREET STATION AND CITY CHAMBERS

Queen Street Station, the starting point of this tour, runs frequent train services to Edinburgh, Dundee and all points north, as well as a suburban service from the Clyde coast to Lanarkshire. Built on the site of a

George Square is a popular meeting place.

quarry in 1842 with a daring curved glass roof, it is Glasgow's oldest station. Beside it, **George Square ❶** began as a muddy hollow in 1781 and developed into a civic meeting place over two centuries. Its beautiful lawns have been replaced with red tarmac, much to the chagrin of office workers who used to sunbathe there at the first blink of sunshine.

The **Millennium Hotel** to the right of the station as you face it was, naturally, a railway hotel, and the BR initials (for 'British Rail') can still be seen above the doorway.

The next office block on the left is best sped past in order to come to the **City Chambers ❷** (Ground Floor only, Mon–Fri 8.30am–5pm; guided tours of whole building, Mon–Fri 10.30am and 2.30pm; free), the towering statement of Glasgow's Victorian confidence, based on the east side of the square. It was opened in 1888 and, according to the architect, was a 'free treatment of the Italian Renaissance'. The ornate front has witnessed momentous events in the square below, including the raising of the hammer and sickle by the Glasgow Soviet in 1919.

The interiors are a riot of marble, mosaic and alabaster. The vaulted ceiling of the entrance hall alone is covered with one and a half million Venetian mosaic tiles. Linger in the entrance hall, where tours begin and excited local schoolchildren often admire the Chambers mosaic coat of arms on the floor, with arms that reflect legends about Glasgow's patron saint, St Mungo. There are four emblems: the bird, tree, bell and fish, as remembered in the following verse:

Here's the Bird that never flew
Here's the Tree that never grew
Here's the Bell that never rang
Here's the Fish that never swam

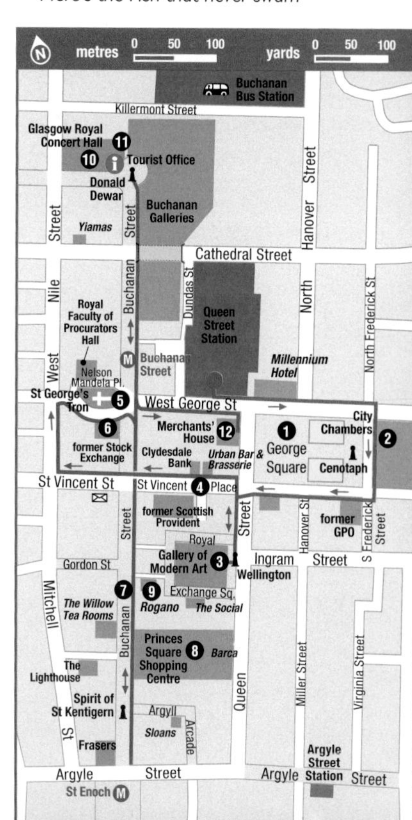

Glasgow Hotel Stories

It was at dinner at the Millennium Hotel in 1941 that Roosevelt's World War II envoy Harry Hopkins pledged American support to Britain against Hitler with the biblical reply: 'Whither thou goest, I will go; and where thou lodgest, I will lodge; thy people shall be my people, and thy God my God.' Winston Churchill, who also had a Central Hotel suite during World War II, nearly choked on his cigar. A Glasgow myth goes that Roy Rogers also had a suite in those grand Central Station lodgings, and rode his horse Trigger up and down the main staircase.

The American envoy – and eloquent speaker – Harry Hopkins.

Granite and marble staircases lead like Escher paintings to the council chambers where the Lord Provost (the Scottish equivalent of Mayor) presides over the city's affairs. There are seats for all 79 councillors, all facing the Lord Provost, his Depute, and the Chief Executive, who are seated behind the mace. If you are interested in visiting while the council is in session you can book a place in the public gallery (for information tel: 0141-287 4005), which looks down on the proceedings, and listen to the lively banter that emanates during debate. Civic functions are regularly held in the great Banqueting Hall, under murals painted by 'Glasgow Boys' Henry, Lavery and Roche, which portray the city's colourful history.

The Cenotaph in front of the City Chambers.

Passing the white, lion-flanked monolith of the **Cenotaph**, where since its unveiling in 1924 people from throughout the city and beyond have congregated to pay tribute to the fallen, the south side of the square begins with the former General Post Office, which has been redeveloped as offices and luxury flats. From here, continue across Hanover Street to the junction with Queen Street.

GALLERY OF MODERN ART

Turning left down Queen Street, past bars and fast-food restaurants, the great pillared hall on the right in Royal Exchange Square is the **Gallery of Modern Art** ❸ (GoMA; tel: 0141-

The much-decorated statue of Wellington outside the GoMA.

287 3050; www.glasgowlife.org.uk; Mon–Wed and Sat 10am–5pm, Thu 10am–8pm, Fri and Sun 11am–5pm; free). Guarded by a statue of Wellington by Baron Marocchetti (which revellers crown most Friday and Saturday nights with a traffic cone), the gallery was previously the Stirling Library. It grew out of a house owned by tobacco baron William Cunningham of Lainshaw, and the huge Corinthian columns at the front and the hall at the rear were added later.

GoMA opened in 1996 to a welter of controversy about its collection. Many critics damned it for populism, but the citizens voted with their feet, and attendance continues to exceed expectations.

It is divided into four galleries and there is a great café in the basement by the GoMA Library. The cavernous ground-floor space retains its columns and original classical features, lending itself to sprawling, bold pieces (see main picture p.66). The upper galleries use natural light wonderfully, and concentrate on group shows that frequently tackle challenging themes.

A striking view of the roof of the Gallery of Modern Art.

In 2009, the exhibition *shOUT* caused a furore in the right-wing press and even stirred up condemnation from the Vatican. The show focused on gay, lesbian, transgender and intersex life – with explicit images created by the likes of Nan Goldin, David Hockney and Robert Mapplethorpe. One exhibit, *Made in God's Image*, in which visitors were invited to add comments to the pages of a Bible, attracted 600 complaints.

ST VINCENT PLACE

Returning up Queen Street and turning left, **St Vincent Place** ❹ opens up an august street of banks and offices faced with the full repertoire of Victorian masonry. The Clydesdale Bank on the north side has bas-reliefs, crouching men and encircled emblems of the towns where the bank has had a presence. Opposite, the former Scottish Provident Building's red sandstone reaches skyward.

Handsome Pubs

Some of Glasgow's gorgeous, solid buildings are now devoted to the Glaswegian passion for having a blether over a drink. **The Counting House** (tel: 0141-225 0160) on the corner of George Square has been converted into a pub and restaurant with splendid interior statuary, cornicing and glass dome above the bar; **The Auctioneers** (tel: 0141-222 2989) in North Court is also a pub and restaurant furbished with the kind of bric-a-brac that used to pass through McTear's showrooms; and **78 St Vincent** (tel: 0141-248 7878) is beautifully lit by the vaulting windows of a former bank, and has an interior reminiscent of Le Chartier restaurant in Paris.

St George's Tron on West George Street.

ST GEORGE'S TRON AND GLASGOW STOCK EXCHANGE

Passing a variety of city shops on the left, the tour turns right into West Nile Street and right again into West George Street. The church in the cen-

The stunning interior of The Counting House pub.

Inside the GoMA, all white and clean lines.

tre of the road is **St George's Tron** ❺, built in 1807 to accommodate the westward movement of the city. It was designed by William Stark, who was also responsible for a jail on Glasgow Green and a lunatic asylum. The Tron has a long tradition of being at the evangelical wing of the Church of Scotland: Tom Allan was a key figure in the Scottish evangelical movement of the mid-20th century, and if you pop in today you are sure to be greeted by an enthusiastic minister.

On the north side of the square, Nelson Mandela Place, is the former Old Athenaeum which, on opening in 1888, offered classes in science, philosophy and literature to more than 1,000 students. It now houses the Hard Rock Café. Tucked into the corner is the Royal Faculty of Procurators Hall, with the heads of law lords carved on the window arches. On the other side of the square is the early French Gothic extravagance of the former **Glasgow Stock Exchange** ❻ building, which brings to mind the London Law Courts and is a rather rare flight of fancy amid the solidity of its surroundings. It, too, now houses shops.

BUCHANAN STREET

The wide avenue of **Buchanan Street** ❼, the city's most prestigious shopping arena, stretches southward. It starts at Argyle Street, with Frasers on its domed corner site, and leads up a Victorian canyon fronted by design-

A mix of architectural styles off Buchanan Street.

er names. In the pedestrianised centre is the winged *Spirit of St Kentigern* statue. Buskers, from lone evangelists to full string quartets, provide daily entertainment.

Shopping

Further along on the right is the **Argyll Arcade**, an enclosed walkway lined with jewellers' shops, which leads in a right-angle back to Argyle Street. Nearby is the entrance to **Princes Square** ❽, a beautiful mall packed with trendy boutiques and bars on several levels. It is best entered via the central escalator, past *trompe l'oeil* paintings of such luminaries as Sir Thomas Lipton, Keir Hardie and John Logie Baird.

On the top floor, while looking down at the mosaic of the central well, you will not fail to notice the huge **Foucault's Pendulum**, a replica of the device by which Jean-Bernard-Léon Foucault proved the rotation of the Earth in the dome of the Pantheon in Paris in 1851. The centre is a veritable shopaholic's dream, with the presence of top names in fashion such as Vivienne Westwood, as well as upmarket high-street chains such as Ted Baker, while the upper floors have a range of cafés, bars and restaurants including Sugar Dumplin, Barca Tapas and Cava Bar, October and Cranachan.

It's a wonderful building to visit and especially welcome during a rainy spell of Glasgow weather – not uncommon of course – as the twinkly lights, inviting shops and top-floor cafés provide a cheery diversion before you brave the elements again.

Pick of the Shops

COS
Princes Square; tel: 0141-202 7480; Mon–Fri 10am–7pm, Sat 9am–6pm, Sun 11am–5pm.
The fashion editors' high-street favourite, COS sells stylish yet simple clothes for men and women with a focus on sharp, minimalist lines and classic wardrobe must-haves.

Tam Shepherd's Trick Shop
33 Queen Street; tel: 0141-221 2310; Mon–Sat 10am–5.30pm (until 6pm Fri).
Practical jokes, magic tricks, wigs and masks fill this fun emporium which inspired Louise Welsh's novel *The Bullet Trick*.

Tiso
129 Buchanan Street; tel: 0141-248 4877; Mon–Sat 9.30am–5.30pm (until 7.30pm Thu), Sun 11am–5pm.
With Glasgow being in such close proximity to Loch Lomond and the Trossachs (see page 104), Tiso is a useful stopoff for those in search of outdoor gear. There are five floors to trawl through!

Vivienne Westwood
Unit 3, Princes Square; tel: 0141-222 2643; Mon–Sat 9.30am–5.30pm (until 6pm Sat), Sun noon–5pm.
The British fashion icon brings her great mix of punk, tartan, bondage and theatricality to the swanky surroundings of Princes Square.

Have your pick of fake moustaches at Tam Shepherd's Trick Shop.

The ornate Glasgow Stock Exchange building.

Galleries and Royal Concert Hall

Opposite Princes Square on Mitchell Lane is the very cool Lighthouse, Scotland's Centre for Design and Architecture, which features a Mackintosh Interpretation Centre. Back on Buchanan Street, the shopping choice is wide, from chic labels and brands including Hugo Boss, L'Occitane and Apple. Weary shoppers can stop at The **Willow Tea Rooms** (see page 99), which is a replica based on the many remnants of Charles Rennie Mackintosh's original restaurant designs owned by the City Council, or **Rogano** ❾, a splendid Art Deco shellfish restaurant in the passageway leading to Royal Exchange Square.

As you head past Graham Tiso, Hobbs and The White Company and back across St Vincent Street to the Stock Exchange, the view northwards takes in the **Buchanan Galleries**, an enormous shopping complex development that encom-

Out and about on Buchanan Street.

The Willow Tea Rooms re-create the designs by Charles Rennie Mackintosh for a restaurant at the turn of the century.

passes several city blocks and a pedestrianised area at the **Glasgow Royal Concert Hall** ⑩ (tel: 0141-353 8000; www.glasgowconcerthalls.com), the city's main venue for classical concerts. The centrepiece here is a statue of the late Donald Dewar, credited as the driving force behind the new Scottish Parliament.

VISITSCOTLAND INFORMATION CENTRE

On the corner of Sauchiehall Street and Buchanan Street is the **Glasgow VisitScotland Information Centre** ⑪ (tel: 0845 859 1006; Apr–Sep Mon–Sat 9am–6pm, Sun 10am–5pm, Oct–Mar Mon–Sat 9am–6pm, Sun noon–4pm). It's a great place to pick up leaflets and maps, and experts can provide inspiring local and national information. They will also book accommodation or tours on your behalf, locally and across Scotland. You can purchase tickets for the local sightseeing bus trips to different destinations in Scotland, as well as various local and national attractions and events. On sale are a range of Scottish gifts that include those by Gillian Kyle and Harris Tweed, plus maps, guide books, postcards, stamps and kitsch souvenirs.

MERCHANTS' HOUSE

Returning along West George Street to George Square, the oriel-windowed **Merchants' House** ⑫ (not open to the public) reflects the confidence and self-importance of the guilds that

Rogano is an Art Deco tour de force and a memorably decadent dining experience.

created it. Housing the Chamber of Commerce, which is the second oldest in the world after the one in New York, it hosts occasional concerts (see local press for details).

The original Merchants' Hall, constructed around 1600, acted as a meeting place for merchants and as an almshouse for merchants and their families who had fallen on hard times. The Hall was rebuilt in the 1650s to a design by Sir William Bruce of Kinross, who would later be architect to King Charles II. The old layout consisted of ground-floor lodgings for old couples and facilities for pensioners. The imposing present-day building was opened in 1877, according to a design by John Burnet; his son added two storeys in 1908. The Merchants' House of Glasgow bought part of the estate of Wester Craigs in 1650, and funded the landscaping of the city's grand Necropolis in the 1830s.

Eating Out

Barca
Level 2, Princes Square; tel: 0141-248 6555; www.barcatapas.co.uk; daily noon–midnight.
Wonderful traditional Spanish tapas such as prawns in chilli sauce and chorizo sausage or a full paella of meat or fish (two people sharing), as well as a cava bar just for drinks. £

Darcy's
The Courtyard, Princes Square; tel: 0141-226 4309; www.darcysglasgow.co.uk; daily lunch and dinner.
For some café-style panache in the Princes Square shopping centre, book a leather booth at this ground-floor joint. As well as decent coffee, the varied menu includes Scots Angus burgers and pan-fried seabass. £

Rogano
11 Exchange Place; tel: 0141-248 4055; www.roganoglasgow.com; daily lunch and dinner.
Glasgow's homage to the days of ocean liners and cocktails exudes 1930s glamour and offers top-class service. It's also the place for oysters. Dress up. £££

Sloans
62 Argyll Arcade, 108 Argyle Street; tel: 0141-221 8886; www.sloansglasgow.com; daily lunch and dinner.
An Edwardian-style pub-restaurant with Grade A-listed interiors including a grand ballroom and a cosy, snug bar. Serves simple British cuisine. £

The Social
27 Royal Exchange Square; tel: 0845-166 6016; www.thesocialglasgow.co.uk; daily lunch and dinner.
A swanky bar full of suits by day and dressed-up Glaswegians by night with an interesting brasserie menu that includes pasta dishes, juicy steaks and veggie-friendly options. There is also a decent brunch menu at weekends. £

Urban Bar & Brasserie
23–25 St Vincent Place; tel: 0141-248 5636; www.urbanbrasserie.co.uk; daily lunch and dinner.
This stylish bar-restaurant, housed in the former Bank of England HQ, has a regularly changing brasserie menu with excellent fish and meat creations. Perennial favourite is the fish soup. ££

Yiamas
16–20 Bath Street; tel: 0141-353 1386; Tue–Sat lunch and dinner.
A basic Greek tavern serving authentic meals from its open kitchen. The Greek owners really bring out the flavour in dishes such as giros and moussaka. £

Steep St Vincent Street.

Tour 5

Going West

This 1¼-mile (2km) walk follows architecturally fascinating St Vincent Street to the historic Mitchell Library, then on to the cutting-edge CCA arts centre – all in half a day

The city has been moving west since medieval times, and, since the more prosperous were the first to decamp, the buildings become noticeably more ornate. Starting the route at the junction of Hope Street and St Vincent Street, the Victorian offices spiral upwards in ever more detailed flights of the stonemason's fancy. Looking south, the clock tower of the Grand Central Hotel looms above Central Station, the main link to the south, in an austere welcome.

Highlights

- St Vincent Street Free Church of Scotland
- The King's Theatre
- Mitchell Library
- Tenement House
- CCA: Centre for Contemporary Arts

UP AND DOWN ST VINCENT STREET

St Vincent Street, named after the naval battle at Cabo de São Vicente, is a thoroughfare devoted to Mammon, so it is fitting that its long incline is crowned with one of Scotland's finest temples to God. On the way up the hill, there's a beguiling mix of imposing neoclassical, Art Nouveau, Art Deco and modernist buildings including: the old **Phoenix Assurance building** (1913) in American Classical style at No. 78, the eccentric **Hatrack** (1902) with its rich red sandstone, stained glass and spiky lead roof at No. 142–144, and the elegant 1929-built Royal **Sun Alliance Building** at No. 200, with its angular Art Deco statue added in the 1930s.

St Vincent Street Free Church of Scotland ❶ is the best remaining example of the work of Alexander 'Greek' Thomson (1817–75). Thomson, paradoxically, is famous for being Glasgow's 'forgotten architect', forever in the shadow of Charles Rennie Mackintosh (see page 94). Like Mackintosh, he wanted to design every detail of a commission, down to the decorations on the walls. This is the only one of his three city churches still intact, and it has been added to the World Monument Watch for endangered buildings. Light from enormous windows bathes the sumptuous interior, and a recently repaired tower, which recalls India rather than Greece, dominates Blythswood Hill.

On the right, slightly further down the hill, the needle spire of **St Columba's Gaelic Church** soars heaven-wards. It has its roots in the influx of Highlanders who flocked to the city in the 18th and 19th centuries after the so-called Clearances, when landlords evicted crofters to make way for sheep.

Alexander Thomson's St Vincent Street Free Church of Scotland.

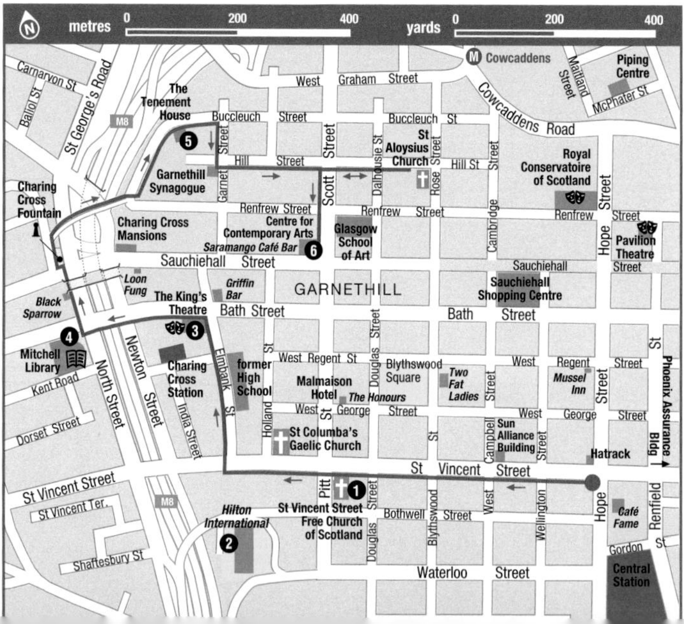

The western end of St Vincent Street is enveloped by the roar of the traffic on the M8, which cuts through an underpass on its way to Edinburgh. The marble and mirrored glass tower on the left is the **Hilton International** ❷, built in 1990 and once state of the art, but now looking a bit tired inside and out.

TOWARDS MITCHELL LIBRARY

As you turn right into Elmbank Street, the white building on the right is the former **High School**, with statues of Galileo, Cicero, Homer and James Watt. The school dates back to the 15th century, but it has gradually moved west from its original home and is now situated in more space in Anniesland. Today, the buildings are occupied by council offices. On the corner of Elmbank Crescent, the ornate grey-stone building provides rehearsal rooms for Scottish Opera and Scottish Ballet, two of Scotland's most prestigious companies. It used to be the home of the Institute of Shipbuilders and Engineers, and a bronze plaque just inside the entrance pays tribute to the engineers who went down at their posts on the *Titanic* in 1912.

The King's Theatre ❸ (tel: 0844-871 7648), on the corner of Elmbank Street and Bath Street, was the most fashionable Glasgow venue of the Edwardian age. Built in 1904, with a lion mascot in stone above the entrance, it provides a stage for a variety of shows, catering for most ages and tastes. Expect lots of West End-style musicals – such as *Legally Blond* and *Sister Act* – stand-up comedy shows from the likes of Frankie Boyle and Paddy McGuinness, and the odd ballet production or popular musical extravaganza thrown in for good measure. The **Griffin Bar** opposite the theatre dates from the same period. Known as The King's Arms up until 1969, the refurbished (2008) Griffin is a 'B' listed building with original wooden interiors, window panels and lead work. It's worth popping your head in and ordering a pint and a sneaky wee dram to take a closer gan-

The Mitchell Library is the largest of its kind in Europe.

Life in the Auld Tenements

A tour around the 1892-built Tenement House makes for a thought-provoking and fun visit for adults and children alike. It's not often you can hear the tick-tock of the grandfather clock while poring over old labels and utensils around the basic kitchen range. Eyes and minds wander through the assorted contents – old jam jars, food tins and household bills – and back in time to a much simpler cramped existence.

The Tenement House reveals Glaswegian life in years gone by.

der at the main bar, with its handsome tiled floor and back-to-back rows of fixed leather seats.

Mitchell Library

Heading left down Bath Street through a canyon of modern offices, you will see the splendid dome of the **Mitchell Library** ❹ (www.glasgowlife.org.uk; Mon–Thu 9am–8pm, Fri–Sat 9am–5pm), adorned with its statue of Minerva and rising above the motorway traffic. It was the legacy of tobacco heir Stephen Mitchell, and, after homes in Ingram Street and Miller Street, the collection moved to the present site in 1911. It is now the biggest public reference library in Europe, and its comprehensive Glasgow Room is a boon and a blessing to those with an interest in the city. Take a peek inside and the friendly janitor may direct you along the handsome marble and dark-wood lined corridors. There's a good little café next to the modern IT suite amid miles of crazy, lurid geometric carpet and books.

The Mitchell Library has fabulous, free resources for those looking to research family history or anyone just curious about the city's past. Level 5 and the Family History Section is manned by knowledgeable staff who help people from all over the world delve into records such as the Glasgow newspaper archive (starting in 1715), censuses, war deaths, parish registers and monumental inscriptions. Leaf through the trade directories to discover intriguing old professionals such as the phrenologist who studied the skull's lumps and bumps to determine personality traits.

The ornate King's Theatre stages a wide range of productions.

The Black Sparrow pub.

BACK EAST TO TENEMENT HOUSE

Head up North Street past the excellent **Black Sparrow** pub and across Sauchiehall Street, to where the ornate fountain at Charing Cross may not have the cachet of Pisa, but the drunken angle at which it leans is every bit as dramatic. Walking north, head for the pedestrian bridge that spans the motorway. A pause here affords a close-up look at the graceful red-sandstone curve of Charing Cross Mansions and, on the left, the turrets, arched windows and balconies of St George's Mansions, both testament to the graciousness into which tenement living evolved.

The CCA is known for staging an eclectic programme.

It pays to keep this Edwardian splendour in mind on the walk from the end of the bridge on the path up through grass and trees to **The Tenement House** ❺ (www.nts.org.uk; Mar–Oct daily 1–5pm, extended hours Jul & Aug). It lies at the end of the walkway at 145 Buccleuch Street and is fascinating because it offers a glimpse of tenement life. It was the home for 50 years of a spinster who changed nothing in her 'wally close' (tiled common stairway). The gaslit parlour, black range and rosewood piano are, as the National Trust for Scotland, which now runs it says, 'a sure sign of gentility'.

Returning along Buccleuch Street, turn right into Garnet Street and then left into Hill Street: this was for many years the heart of the ethnic Chinese community. On the other side, Italy is recalled by the domed grandeur of **St Aloysius Church**, which is attached to the Jesuit school further up the street.

CCA – CENTRE FOR CONTEMPORARY ARTS

Turn left down Scott Street to hit Sauchiehall Street, renowned for its vibrant nightlife, music venues and bars. At No. 350 stands the superb **Centre for Contemporary Arts** ❻ (CCA; tel: 0141-352 4900; www.cca-glasgow.com; gallery Tue–Sat 11am–6pm, Sun noon–6pm; free), which has six exhibitions a year and mounts an eclectic programme. Alongside the changing visual arts exhibitions there are interactive performance-based art workshops, cinema screenings (lots of independent films, shorts, documentaries and classics) and a superb programme of musical events, ranging from improvised soundscapes to traditional Gaelic nights and dance-focussed DJ sets. Visiting performers and artists from all over the world mean you never know what strange delights might be on the bill. The Saramago Café Bar is a wonderful space and has a stylish terrace with some of Glasgow's best weekend music events.

Eating Out

The Black Sparrow
241 North Street; tel: 0141-221 5530; www.theblacksparrow.co.uk; daily noon–9pm.
Stylish bar with decent food menu that includes mains such as lamb tagine and pork belly with honey and chilli glaze. Also serves up a selection of burgers and pizzas. £

Café Fame
127 Hope Street; tel: 0141-258 3838; daily breakfast, lunch and dinner.
Laid-back Italian café serving authentic classics, including recipes passed down through generations, and excellent coffee. The elegant space lives up to its name – images of celebrities adorn the walls. £

The Honours
Malmaison Hotel, 278 West George Street; tel: 0141-572 1001; daily lunch and dinner.
Down in the moodily lit basement with stunning domed ceilings, Martin Wishart launched his brasserie at The Malmaison in 2014. The menu features a mix of traditional and modern French cuisine. ££

Loon Fung
417 Sauchiehall Street; tel: 0141-332 1240; www.loonfungglasgow.co.uk; daily lunch and dinner.
Long-established but still admirable Cantonese cuisine, much frequented by the Chinese community. £

Mussel Inn
157 Hope Street; tel: 0843-289 2283; www.mussel-inn.com; daily lunch and dinner.
Features the best of west coast seafood – oysters, scallops, prawns and, of course, mussels. ££

Saramago Café Bar
CCA, 30 Sauchiehall Street; tel: 0141-352 4920; daily lunch and dinner.
A vegetarian venue offering a variety of mezze dishes, salads and mains such as beetroot and mushroom bourguignon, served in a wonderfully airy enclosed courtyard. £

Two Fat Ladies
118a Blythswood Street; tel: 0141-847 0088; www.twofatladiesrestaurant.com; daily lunch and dinner.
An elegant dining room – usually packed – serving seafood creations such as seared scallops, sea bream and ling, plus enticing desserts. ££

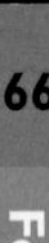

D.I.Y. Glasgow

Glasgow's music and arts scenes have a D.I.Y. spirit at their heart and, for many, the city's rough-hewn edge makes a refreshing change from London, Paris, New York and Venice

The flux of Glasgow's riverside post-industrial landscape – all old decrepit warehouses rubbing alongside sleek, contemporary architecture – seems to flow into the city's creative population. Likewise its indie music labels eschew the corporate and bland, creating a vibrant scene with lots of great bands and venues.

AN ART LEGACY

Despite the devastating fire that ravaged the Charles Rennie Mackintosh-designed **Glasgow School of Art** (GSA) building, the institution still whirs with the comings and goings of students and artists. It was the home of the influential *fin-de-siècle* Glasgow Group of modern artists – which included Charles Rennie Mackintosh – and also boasts celebrated alumni such as Alasdair Gray, Ian Hamilton Finlay, and contemporary artists Jim Lambie, Roddy Buchanan and Simon Starling.

Glasgow's D.I.Y. spirit flourished in the late 1970s and early 1980s, when the city was deep in recession and blighted by sectarian violence. New Glasgow Boys and Girls took over warehouse spaces and set up gallery collectives, the most influential being **Transmission** in 1983 (www.transmissiongallery.org). By 1996 contemporary art was part of the main-

A work by Jim Lambie at GoMA.

stream and Glasgow got itself a grand building to showcase its artists: the **Gallery of Modern Art (GoMA)**. Arts hubs CCA (Centre for Contemporary Arts), **Tramway** and **Tron-gate** 103 followed.

Both the **Glasgow Art Fair** and **Glasgow International Festival** – the city's answer to the Venice Biennale – attract an international crowd. The impetus continues. The GSA's campus redevelopment showcases the state-of-the-art Reid building and visitor centre, and restoration of the Mackintosh building is underway. Merchant City is a buzzing cultural quarter hosting an annual festival.

A THRIVING MUSIC SCENE

Glasgow's music scene was born out of bedroom obsession with exotic sounds. In 1979, the D.I.Y. punk ethos of Postcard Records squeezed Orange Juice and Edwyn Collins from bedroom to Top of the Pops. The city's Gaelic roots, flirtation with Country and popular Americana can be heard in the uplifting Motown beats and West Coast jangly pop of many Glasgow bands. Teenage Fan Club recast the sunshine harmonies of the Byrds and Big Star in late 1980s Glasgow. Some have an art-school sensibility, such as Franz Ferdinand, while Electronica DJ duo Slam mined Teutonic beats and Detroit techno music, founding Soma Quality Recordings in 1991.

A good place to start is the independent record shop-café-venue **Mono** (www.monocafebar.com), part owned by Pastels frontman Stephen McRobbie. It stages film nights, gigs and other cultural events, including the odd appearance by artist David Shrigley.

Alongside big venues including the **Scottish Exhibition and Conference Centre** (SECC; see page 12), there are many intimate venues and bars where Glasvegas, The Fratellis and Camera Obscura regularly appear. Top names include the legendary **Barrowland Ballroom** (www.glasgow-barrowland.com/ballroom). O2ABC (www.o2abcglasgow.co.uk) and **King Tut's Wah Wah Hut** (www.kingtuts.co.uk) host established indie bands. **Nice N' Sleazy** (www.nicensleazy.com) and **Stereo** (www.stereocafebar.com) showcase up-and-coming acts. **Òran Mór** (www.oran-mor.co.uk) and **The Glad Café** (www.thegladcafe.co.uk) in Southside are also on the music map.

An exhibit at the Kelvingrove Art Gallery and Museum.

Tour 6

From Kelvingrove to the Clyde

This half-day, 2.5-mile (4km) stroll around the green surroundings of Kelvingrove Art Gallery and Museum leads to museums and landmarks on the Clyde waterfront

This walk is a welcome escape from the noisy M8 and is a journey to the heart of Glasgow's Victorian achievements as part of the British Empire. Calm prevails along curving streets lined with handsome Victorian sandstone terraced houses, and the twisting paths around leafy Kelvingrove Park lead to the impressive Kelvingrove Art Gallery and Museum. Then it's all modern achievement with the new architectural highlights of 21st-century Glasgow.

Highlights

- Lobey Dosser
- Kelvingrove Park
- Kelvingrove Art Gallery and Museum
- Riverside Museum
- Glasgow Science Centre

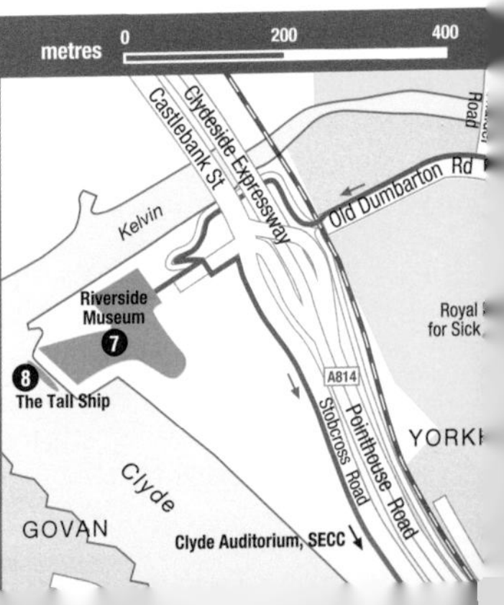

The beloved statue of Lobey Dosser.

LOBEY DOSSER AND PARK CIRCUS

Glasgow is peppered with bronze memorials commemorating the cream of Queen Victoria's empire, but the statue, that holds the fondest place in the hearts of Glaswegians, is of a mustachioed sheriff astride a two-legged horse. It is to be found at the start of this walk on the corner of Woodlands Road, which runs west from Charing Cross and Park Drive.

Lobey Dosser ❶, as the statue is called, was the creation of newspaper

West End Shopping

The West End has an interesting array of independent shops, most of which are just north and west of this route on Byres Road and Great Western Road. Among the foodie places **IJ Mellis** Cheesemonger (492 Great Western Road; tel: 0141-339 8998; Mon–Wed 9.30am–6pm, Thu–Fri 9am–7pm, Sat 9am–6pm, Sun 11am–5pm), stocks cheese from across Europe, with a superb Scottish selection. **The Glasgow Vintage Co.** at 453 Great Western Road (tel: 0141-338 6633; Mon–Sat 11am–6pm, Sun 11–5pm) specialises in vintage wear for all the family. Nearby the **Nancy Smillie Jewellery Studio** (425 Great Western Road; tel: 0141-357 1001; Mon–Tue 10am–5.30pm, Wed–Sat 9.30am–5.30pm, Sun 11.30–5pm) stocks jewellery – many pieces by local Scottish designers – accessories and bags.

Trendy Glasgow Vintage Co.

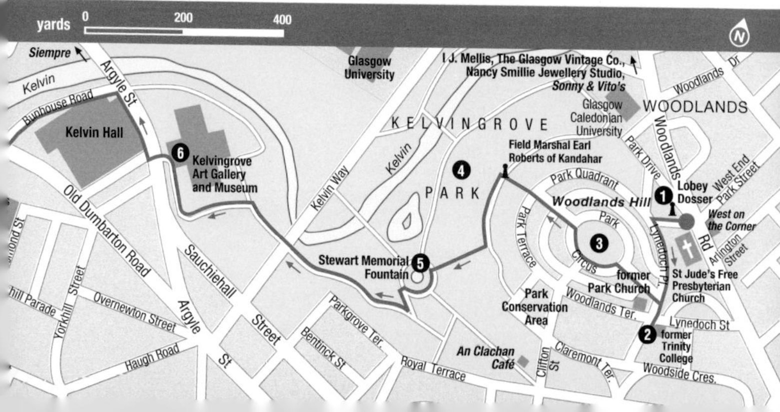

cartoonist Bud Neill who, more than anyone before or since, captured the city's sharp but skewed sense of humour. Regulars in the **Halt Bar**, now known as West on the Corner, across the road were instrumental in raising the public subscription in 1992 to the memory of the Sheriff of Calton Creek and his masked adversary Rank Bajin. The question 'What was the name of Lobey Dosser's horse?' has sparked a thousand pub arguments, and knowing the answer (El Fideldo) will give you instant credibility with Glaswegians.

Leaving the mix of antiques shops and restaurants in Woodlands Road, the route runs from the spire of St Jude's Free Presbyterian Church up through the greenery of Woodlands Hill and left into Lynedoch Place. This wide street leads to an area of flats and offices dominated by the Italianate towers of **Trinity College** ❷, formerly the college of the Free Church and now converted into much sought-after flats. Along with the lonely white tower of the Park Parish Church – the rest of it was demolished in the late 1960s – they form a dramatic focus for the city skyline.

A statue of a scholar on a bridge over the River Kelvin.

Strollers in Kelvingrove Park.

Along the Kelvin Walkway

There are lots of fabulous opportunities for cycling and walking in and around Kelvingrove Park and the Botanic Gardens. One less well-known route follows the Kelvin Walkway and links up with the Forth and Clyde Canal towpath at the Kelvin Aqueduct – an impressive feat of 18th-century engineering and architecture, which was once the largest functioning aqueduct in Europe. Ask at the tourist office for detailed maps and consult the Ordnance Survey Explorer map 342.

A handy marker denotes the Kelvin Walkway.

Turn right into Park Circus Place and enter the splendid oval of **Park Circus ❸**, with its air of Victorian elegance. The grand curving terraces rising to a bluff above the River Kelvin were designed as private housing for the emergent middle classes by Charles Wilson (1810–63) and can justly be regarded as his masterpiece.

KELVINGROVE PARK

They lead to **Kelvingrove Park ❹**, the first custom-built park in the city and site of three great International Exhibitions, in 1888, 1901 and 1911, which proudly proclaimed Glasgow's contribution to the British Empire.

The Victorians viewed public parks as the lungs of their smoky cities, allowing their workers the physically and morally beneficial effects of clean air and uplifting scenery. **Glasgow Green** (see page 31) was the only public space in the city until 1846, when a grand plan was proposed by the city council to create three huge sculpted parklands – **Kelvingrove** in the west, **Alexandra Park** in the east and **Queen's Park** (see page 87) in the south – under the hand of designer Sir Joseph Paxton, of Crystal Palace fame. The city now boasts more than 70 parks, and although the recreations reflect Victorian tastes – boating ponds, playgrounds, putting and bowling – the work of the inventive and industrious Parks Department has given each its own character.

The entrance to Kelvingrove Park is guarded by a spectacular statue of

A Trinity College tower in the Park district.

Field Marshal Earl Roberts of Kandahar (1832–1914), surrounded by the bas-relief trappings of his Indian campaigns. There is a similar statue of the field marshal in Calcutta. The park itself is a fine example of the ornamental pleasure garden, with winding paths and wide boulevards. As you descend into the park, the main thoroughfare and bridge are marked by a memorial to the officers and men of the Highland Light Infantry who fell in the 'South African War' or Boer War (1899–1902). Turning left here, the road leads through dappled shade to the extravagance of the **Stewart Memorial Fountain ❺**, a tribute to the Lord Provost who, in 1855, finally managed to secure a supply of pure water to the city from Loch Katrine in the Trossachs.

Turning right past the skateboard park and the duck ponds, the tour emerges onto the Kelvin Way, and a bridge cornered by four groups of bronzes representing peace and war, commerce and industry, shipping and navigation, and prosperity and progress. They were badly damaged by German bombers in 1941 and restored by sculptor Benno Schotz 10 years later.

The Stewart Memorial Fountain in Kelvingrove Park.

In the Kelvingrove Art Gallery and Museum.

KELVINGROVE ART GALLERY

The path opposite the park gate leads to the red-sandstone grandeur of **Kelvingrove Art Gallery and Museum ❻** (tel: 0141-276 9599; www.glasgowlife.org.uk; Mon–Thu and Sat 10am–5pm, Fri and Sun 11am–5pm; free), a superb repository of one of the finest civic collections in Europe. The gallery had its origins in the paintings of Trades House Deacon Convenor Archibald McLellan, which the city acquired in 1854 along with his gallery in Sauchiehall Street. The need to house these and other displays led to the 1888 Exhibition – a mammoth event attended by Queen Victoria and nearly 6 million of her subjects – and the profits were used as pump-priming money

Some say that the Gallery was built the 'wrong way round', because the main entrance is from Kelvingrove Park, while most visitors enter from Argyle Street.

for the new building. The project was conceived on a breathtaking scale, with its twin towers, which shelter a massive bronze of St Mungo, facing the lacework spire of Glasgow University, and the other side leading down a grand staircase onto sunken gardens. Visited by over 1 million people each year, the Kelvingrove reopened its impressive interior in 2007 after a £27.9 million, three-year refurbishment. Its enormous galleries are arranged around two naturally lit halls on either side of the Great Hall, which has an immense Lewis pipe organ still used for recitals.

Kids at Kelvingrove

The Kelvingrove Art Gallery and Museum has much to appeal to children. Glaswegian visitors, young and old alike, wander around excitedly and open-jawed, taking in myriad exhibitions, lifelike scale models of animals and the Spitfire LA68 (City of Glasgow Squadron), hanging from the ceiling of the west court. As well as the child-friendly exhibits there are Discovery Centres (info: 0141-276 9505) dedicated to art, environment and history, while the Centre of New Enlightenment (TCoNE; info: 0141-276 9506), in the Campbell Hunter Education Wing, offers interactive educational adventures for young people aged 10 to 14 years.

The Spitfire LA68 is suspended above the west court.

Riverside Museum streetscene.

Kelvingrove's Art Collections
The collection, which includes more than 8,000 objects over three floors and many interactive displays, also features many 17th-century Dutch, French Impressionist and post-Impressionist paintings. Rembrandt's *Man in Armour*, Millet's *Going to Work* and Dalí's *Christ of St John of the Cross* are particular favourites. The Glasgow School, in the forefront of the departure from classical tradition, and the Scottish Colourists are well represented, and among the 3,000 oils and 12,500 drawings and prints are works by Rubens, Pissarro, Van Gogh, Degas, Matisse and Monet. A gallery dedicated to Charles Rennie Mackintosh and the Glasgow Style is also popular. Within the walls of this cultural treasure trove, visitors to the West Wing will find a World War II Spitfire hanging from the ceiling and Sir Roger, a stuffed elephant that was once a resident of Glasgow Zoo.

Leaving from the west end of the art gallery, past the 'machine-gun Tommy' war memorial, cross the street to the **Kelvin Hall** (tel: 0141-276 1450), which for many years was Glasgow's foremost exhibition centre, fondly remembered for its annual carnival and circus, complete with elephants and their distinctive aroma. Built in 1927, it served for 60 years – including war service as a barrage balloon factory – before its functions were transferred to the Scottish Exhibition and Conference Centre next to the Clyde. It is undergoing a £60 million redevelopment and due to open in summer 2016 with state-of-the-art facilities including a cultural hub and community sports centre.

RIVERSIDE MUSEUM AND THE TALL SHIP

From Argyle Street turn left down Bunhouse Road and then right on to Old Dumbarton Road. Continue to the end of the road, under the railway bridge and take the underpass beneath the Expressway to reach the impressive sight of the **Riverside Museum** ❼ (tel: 0141-287 2720; www.glasgowlife.org.uk; Mon–Thu and Sat 10am–5pm, Fri and Sun 11am–5pm; free). This striking multi-million-pound transport museum, designed by Zaha Hadid, opened in 2011 and has quickly become one of the UK's top ten attractions. More than 3,000 objects trace the history of transport, most of them relating to Scotland, from a velodrome of

The award-winning Riverside Museum at Pointhouse Quay was developed for the Museum of Transport.

bicycles suspended from the ceiling to a wall of classic cars spanning the decades to a new motorbike wall. Most popular, particularly with children, are the old trams, bus and subway carriage – climb aboard to get a real sense of travel in days gone by. Continuing the nostalgic theme, there are two areas recreating streetscapes from the 1890s to the 1960s with replicas of specialist shops and pubs.

To the rear of the museum is **The Tall Ship** ❽ (tel: 0141-357 3699; www.thetallship.com; daily Feb–Oct 10am–5pm, Nov–Jan 10am–4pm; free). The restored *Glenlee*, a Clyde-built three-masted barque, sailed the globe from the 1890s to the 1920s – she made journeys as far afield as Argentina, Australia and Japan – before becoming a naval training ship. The four decks can now be explored to find out what life was like on board. Visit the crews' cabins, galley, hospital and map room.

Next to The Tall Ship, **Seaforce** (tel: 0141-221 1070; www.seaforce.co.uk) runs exciting powerboat rides along the Clyde, weather permitting.

ALONG THE CLYDE

Return to the front of the Riverside Museum and follow Stobcross Road, running parallel with the busy Pointhouse Road, around to the SECC and the Clyde Auditorium. Unless you're attending a conference or a concert at the **Scottish Exhibition and Conference Centre (SECC)** (tel: 0844-395 4000) or the neighbouring **Clyde Auditorium** ❾ (tel: 0141-248 3000) you're unlikely to go inside either of these two colossal buildings. But the architectural splendour – particularly of the latter, known affectionately as the 'Armadillo' – makes

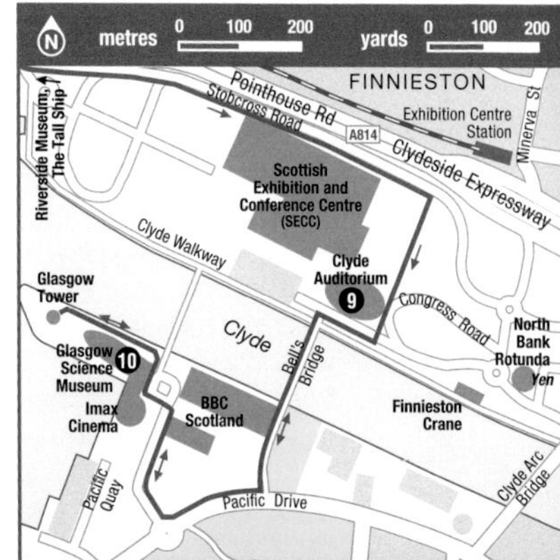

The Finnieston Crane is no longer in active use, but remains as a landmark to Glasgow's industrial heritage.

them must-sees and they have become symbolic of the whole regeneration of Glasgow from the 1980s onwards. The architect Sir Norman Foster took inspiration from this former ship-building area, designing an exterior intended to emulate ships' hulls. On a sunny day, as the light hits the silvery curves, it's a stunning sight. Adjacent to these two buildings is yet another live venue the immense, futuristic SSE Hydro (tel: 0844-395 4000).

As you walk down towards the river along Lancefield Quay, the hulking **Finnieston Crane** comes into view. This huge cantilever crane was in use for more than 50 years as a means of lifting heavy machinery, but it became redundant as industry died out in the city in the 1990s. Today, however, it stands as a dramatic tribute to the great industrial heritage of Glasgow

ACROSS TO PACIFIC QUAY

At Congress Road on the riverfront take the footbridge over the Clyde, looking to your left as you do so to admire the Clyde Arc Bridge, also known as Squinty Bridge to the locals and another great symbol of modern Glasgow.

Turn right onto Pacific Drive then follow the signs to the **Glasgow Science Centre** ⑩ (tel: 0141-420 5000; www.glasgowsciencecentre.org; daily 10am–5pm). The main permanent attraction here is the planetarium, with various different staged exhibits to demonstrate and explain the solar system and the universe by exploring the night skies, but the science halls, with plenty of interactive exhibits for adults and children alike, hold great appeal too.

The Glasgow Tower is the tallest tower in Scotland.

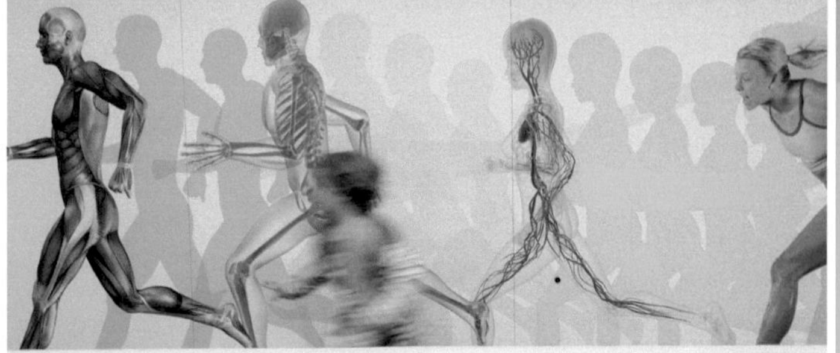

There's plenty for the kids to enjoy at the Glasgow Science Centre.

An IMAX theatre is also on site, while further along the quay and associated with the science centre is the rotating **Glasgow Tower** (Apr–Oct), a 416ft (127m) freestanding edifice. Visitors can ride to the top via a lift for 360-degree views of the city – the tower closed in 2013 due to persistent engineering problems, but it reopened in 2014 with improved safety measures in place.

To return to the city centre, backtrack to the SECC and take bus No. 100 to George Square.

Eating Out

For the best eating options, see the adjoining Tour 7's Eating Out box, page 85. There's a great café in the Kelvingrove Art Gallery. Other options include these deli-cafés and an Oriental restaurant near the SECC:

An Clachan
Kelvingrove Park; tel: 07832-485 668; Mon–Fri 8am–6pm, Sat 9am–6pm, Sun 10am–6pm (closes at 5pm in winter).
This café in the park is particularly pleasant on a fine summer's day. Free-range produce and Fairtrade teas and coffees, plus sandwiches, burgers, soups, home-made bakes and all-day breakfasts are on offer here. £

Siempre Bicycle Café
162 Dumbarton Road Road; tel: 0141-334 2385; www.siemprebicyclecafe.com; Mon–Fri 8am–6pm, Sat–Sun 8.30am–8pm.
Tasty, locally sourced food, complemented by some of the best coffee in town, makes this bicycle-lovers' paradise a great pit stop. £

Sonny & Vito's
52 Park Road; tel: 0141-357 0640; daily 9am–7pm.
A popular and friendly deli just off this tour. It serves excellent home-made sandwiches, pies, tarts, salads and sweet treats including chocolate and chilli brownies. £

Yen
28 Tunnel Street; tel: 0141-847 0330; www.yenrotunda.com; daily lunch and dinner.
Located in the restaurant complex in the lovely rotunda building next to the SECC, Yen specialises in cuisine from the Far East, notably Cantonese, Thai and Japanese dishes. Good-value set-lunch menu. ££

Relaxing in th Botanic Gardens.

Tour 7

West End

Explore the West End's enthralling academic collections, boho Byres Road and the luxuriant Glasgow Botanic Gardens on this 1.3-mile (2km) tour, which will take a minimum of 4 hours

In the hungry 1930s, the young bucks of Govan would cross on the Kelvinhaugh Ferry on a Sunday afternoon and stage their own version of the Latin *paseo* (walking out) with the local girls along the bosky grandeur of the Kelvin Way. And to the boys from the shipyard tenements it must have seemed like a foreign country. This wonderful walk takes in the Kelvin Way – which cuts through Kelvingrove Park – to the fascinating Hunterian art and museum collections on University Avenue, before exploring the boho shops, cafés and restaurants of Byres Road and Ashton Lane. Our jaunt continues to the exotic hothouses of the Botanic Gardens and ends amid the vibrant murals of Glasgow artist Alasdair Gray at the Òran Mór cultural centre.

Highlights

- Kelvin Way
- Wellington Church
- Glasgow University
- Hunterian Museum
- Hunterian Gallery
- Byres Road
- Ashton and Cresswell lanes
- Glasgow Botanic Gardens
- Òran Mór

KELVIN WAY AND GLASGOW UNIVERSITY

Starting at the Sauchiehall Street end of the **Kelvin Way**, the Art Galleries open up on the left and the imposing Gothic front of Glasgow University looms on Gilmorehill. Mature trees canopy the Way after it crosses the bridge with its four dramatic bronzes by Paul R. Montford. On the right is the Kelvingrove bandstand, revamped in 2014 and once more in regular use, while, further along on the left, by an azalea-studded rockery, sit statues of the figures of the great scientist Lord Kelvin (1824–1907) and surgery pioneer Joseph Lister (1827–1912), both in their university robes.

At the end is a cluster of university buildings, with the imposing gothic **Glasgow University Union** straight ahead and the Gilmorehill Centre in a former church on the right. Turning left onto the hill of University Avenue is the gilded gatehouse of **Pearce Lodge ❶**, a remnant of the 17th-century Old College in the city centre, which may be renamed under new guidelines to represent more female alumni of the university.

Uphill on the right is **Wellington Church ❷**, a grand classical structure influenced by the Madeleine in Paris, with 10 massive fluted pillars supporting its portico. Its predecessor stood in Wellington Street in the centre of the city and attracted a well-to-do congregation, evidenced by the fact that its war memorial lists mainly officers, with only a scat-

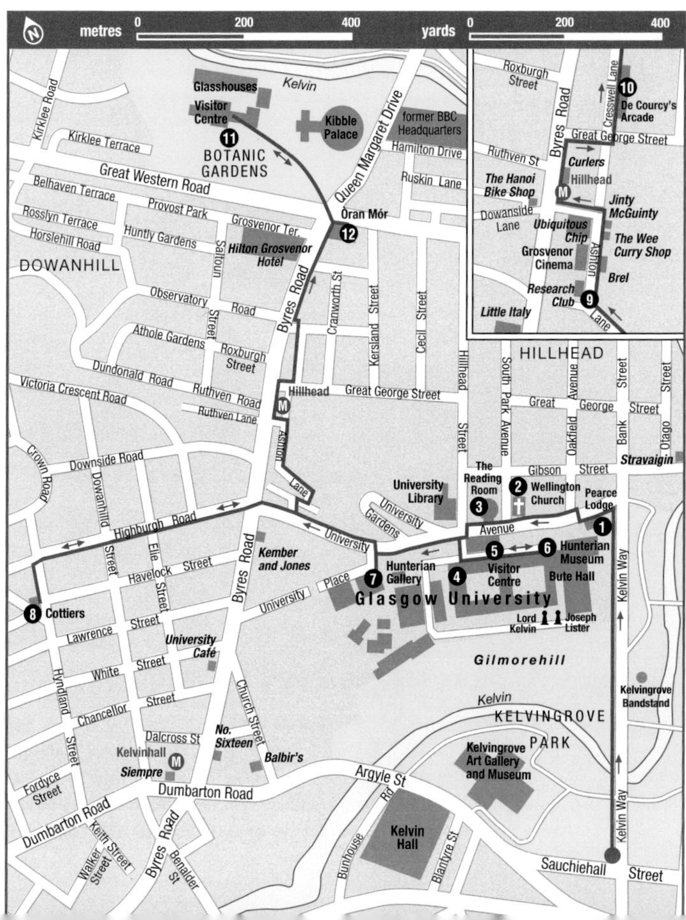

ter of enlisted men. There is a small café in the crypt. Next door is the bright, galleried circle of **The Reading Room** ❸, a quirky but practical study area built in the grounds of Hillhead House, given to the university in 1917 in memory of city merchant Walter MacLellan of Rhu.

Glasgow University ❹, directly across from the Reading Room, is one of the world's great seats of learning, with an outstanding academic history (see page 15) and worldwide influence. The University of Glasgow is the fourth oldest in Britain after St Andrew's, Oxford and Cambridge. In 1870 it moved to its current site, a leaded-windowed building designed by Sir John Gilbert Scott in what he called 'a 13th or 14th century secular style… with Scottish features'. A complex wrought-iron gate carrying the motto *Via Veritas Vita* contains the names of such luminaries as Bute, Kelvin, Lister, Watt, Stair, Adam Smith and Foulis.

Glasgow University is one of the most prestigious in the country.

HUNTERIAN MUSEUM

Just inside the gate is a monument to William and John Hunter, the medical

Inside the fascinating Hunterian Museum.

Lord Kelvin's Inventions

The Hunterian Museum's displays dedicated to Lord Kelvin are a big hit with children. There are lots of hands-on activities, scientific instruments, demonstrations and digital images that bring the work of the Victorian scientist to life. Memorable displays include listening to music from a flame, seeing Kelvin's name lit by high-voltage electricity and testing your capacity to be a human battery.

Imaginative interactive exhibits at the Hunterian Museum.

brothers whose collection forms the basis of the excellent Hunterian Museum, and the award-winning **Visitor Centre** ❺ (Mon–Sat 9.30am–5pm) provides comprehensive information with guided tours of the university (Thu–Sun 2pm).

A staircase by the Visitor Centre leads to the sunlit quadrangles and the contrastingly gloomy cloisters. Here also is the lusciously ornate Bute Hall and the **Hunterian Museum** ❻ (www.gla.ac.uk/hunterian; Tue–Sat 10am–5pm, Sun 11am–4pm; free), Scotland's oldest, which displays the death mask of founder William Hunter. Its splendid galleries house material of great antiquity, from dinosaurs' eggs and rare material from Captain Cook's voyages to ancient coins and a history of the Romans in Scotland. Leaving by the Visitor Centre and turning left, you reach The Square, home to the Principal's residence and the University Chapel.

HUNTERIAN GALLERY

Directly across from the university gatehouse is the **Hunterian Gallery** ❼ (www.gla.ac.uk/hunterian; Tue–Sat 10am–5pm, Sun 11am–4pm; free) and the Mackintosh House within (see page 97), with its internationally famous Whistler collection and works by Rembrandt, Pissarro and Rodin, plus works by the Glasgow Boys and the Scottish Colourists. The museum has put together an impressive collection of contemporary art in recent years through the National Collecting Scheme for Scotland. All the recently acquired

There is a rich collection of Old Masters at the Hunterian Gallery.

Mackintosh's *Porlock Weir* at the Hunterian Gallery.

works have a naturalistic, scientific element that complements the overall collection. The fascinating work of Mark Dion is inspired by the powerful historic role of great museum collections such as the Hunterian's. Other contemporary art highlights worth seeking out are Christine Borland's delicate skulls entitled *Family Conversation Piece: Head of Father* (1998), and Matt Collishaw's strutting peacock, which accompanies the works of Whistler.

The Ubiquitous Chip restaurant is a mainstay of Ashton Lane.

The University Library, which contains more than 2.5 million books and journals, is just a few steps further up Hillhead Street.

BYRES ROAD

Abandoning academia for more hedonistic pleasures, **Byres Road**, at the junction with University Avenue, presents itself as the students' playground. Named after a small *clachan*, or village, which once stood there called Byres of Partick, it is a cosmopolitan mix of restaurants, bars and cafés, and comfortingly solid tenement architecture. Kember and Jones (No. 134), an upmarket deli and café, and The University Café (No. 87) are both excellent eateries on Byres Road. A brief detour up Highburgh Road opposite the junction leads to **Cottiers** 8 (tel: 0141-357 5825; www.cottiers.com), a superb theatre, bar and restaurant in a Victorian Gothic church by architect William Leiper, featuring the beautifully restored stained glass and interior design of Daniel Cottier. It hosts shows by Scottish Opera and Scottish Ballet, as well as experimental companies. Sunday is Family Fun Day, noon–5pm, with kids' films and activities.

Byres Road is lined with cafés.

ASHTON LANE

To return to the route, just before University Avenue reaches Byres Road, turn right into Ashton Road and right again into **Ashton Lane** ❾. This leads down an alley into an explosion of constantly busy bars and restaurants. In less than 100 yds/m, this narrow, cobbled lane offers Brel (tel: 0141-342 4966), with Belgian beer and 'rustic' food, the Grosvenor Cinema with its huge loft café-bar (tel: 0845-166 6028), *Jinty McGuinty*'s packed Irish bar, the Ubiquitous Chip (see page 85) and the Ashoka Indian restaurant (tel: 0141-337 1115); or come back in the evening for cocktails at the cool Research Club (tel: 0141-341 1236). Ruthven Lane close by has antiquarian bookstores and vintage and designer clothes.

De Courcy's Arcade shop sign.

CRESSWELL LANE

Going north up Byres Road past Hillhead Underground and Curlers, an old coaching inn, turn right into Great George Street and then left into **Cresswell Lane** ❿ for De Courcy's Arcade, a warren of stalls selling accessories, jewellery, crafts and retro design. At the end, turn left and then right again into Byres Road to the junction with Great Western Road. On the right is the pyramid spire of the former Kelvinside Parish Church, which has been converted into the Òran Mór music

Shopping Frenzy

Independent boutiques and foodie outlets line Byres Road, while Ruthven Lane and De Courcy's Arcade in Cresswell Lane lure vintage fashion and 20th-century antiques fans. Vintage store **Circa Vintage** (37 Ruthven Lane; tel: 0141-334 6660) bursts with interesting threads, jewellery and curios. Shop for individual styles at Pink Poodle (1813 Byres Road; tel: 0141-357 3344), a well-established boutique for the discerning woman. At No. 382 Byres Road, **Demijohn** (tel: 0141-337 3600) is a self-styled 'liquid deli' full of whiskies, liquors, oils and vinegars. Janet and John (Upper Floor, De Courcy's Arcade, tel: 07331-768 373) is a retail outlet showcasing hand-crafted items from across Scotland. Bookworms will enjoy a visit to **Voltaire & Rousseau** (12–14 Otago Lane; tel: 0141-611 8764), a wonderfully dusty second-hand bookshop, crammed full of finds and collectable first editions.

Inside one of the Kibble Palace glasshouses, at the Botanic Gardens.

centre, restaurant and bar. On the left is the terrace of the **Hilton Grosvenor Hotel**, a quarter-mile repetition of the facades of Venetian palaces. The eastern half was destroyed in a fire in 1978 and rebuilt with glass-reinforced concrete cast from the original pillars.

Directly opposite are the **Glasgow Botanic Gardens** ⓫ (www.glasgowbotanicgardens.com; Gardens: daily 7am–dusk, Glasshouses: 10am–6pm, winter until 4.15pm; free; Garden Tearooms: 10am–4pm), a restful recreation garden relocated from Sauchiehall Street to Kelvinside in 1842, with a herb garden, vegetable garden (highlighting a number of uncommon species) and walks along the Kelvin. The dramatic glasshouses nurture tropical plants. The delicate dome of the Kibble Palace was brought here from the Clyde coast home of John Kibble in 1873. An impressive structure, covering 23,000 sq ft (2,137 sq m), it was originally designed by John Kibble for his home at Coulport on Loch Long in the 1860s, and the components were cast by Walter Macfarlane at his Saracen Foundry in Possilpark.

Òran Mór is a cultural centre in a converted church.

Prime Ministers Benjamin Disraeli and William Gladstone were both installed as rectors of the University of Glasgow under the curved wrought-iron roof in the 1870s – these were the last public events to be staged here before the palace became solely used to house temperate plants. After a £7 million restoration, which involved its complete dismantling and the repair of its rusty parts, the palace was reopened in 2006. The ruins of the Botanic Gardens railway station – opened in 1896 and closed in 1939 – can be seen at the side of the gardens through railings.

Just up Queen Margaret Drive on the right is a building that once housed the women students of Queen Margaret College, as well as the old BBC headquarters, now occupied as offices. The grounds are being redeveloped for housing.

ÒRAN MÓR

Just across from the Glasgow Botanic Gardens on the city-bound section of the Great Western Road is the fine old Kelvinside Parish Church, converted and opened in 2004 as **Òran Mór** ⓬ (meaning 'great melody of life' or 'big song'; www.oran-mor.co.uk). This cultural centre offers bars, venues and an eclectic programme of musical and theatrical events (including the lunchtime 'A Play, A Pie and A Pint' series). Pop in to view the cavernous auditorium and its wonderful murals by artist and novelist Alasdair Gray.

The delicate Kibble Palace at the Glasgow Botanic Gardens.

Return to the city centre by bus from Great Western Road or by Underground from Hillhead (Byres Road) or Kelvinbridge (down Great Western Road).

Eating Out

Balbir's
7 Church Street, West End; tel: 0141-339 7711; www.balbirs.co.uk; daily dinner only.
Don't let the soulless interior fool you. This is an excellent choice for a quick curry packed with flavour and fresh ingredients. £

The Hanoi Bike Shop
8 Ruthven Lane; tel: 0141-334 7165; www.thehanoibikeshop.co.uk; daily lunch and dinner.
Glasgow's only Vietnamese restaurant serves delightful street food in a room with bicycles hanging from the ceiling. It's quirky, and the food is very tasty and authentic. £

Little Italy
205 Byres Road; tel: 0141-339 6287; www.littleitalyglasgow.com; daily breakfast, lunch and dinner.
This popular Italian does takeaways and eat-in pizzas, pasta dishes and a good selection of cakes. £

No. Sixteen
16 Byres Road; tel: 0141-339 2544; www.number16.co.uk; daily lunch and dinner.
No. Sixteen serves impressive cuts of fish and meat, including fillet of trout and slow-cooked belly of pork, with imaginative accompaniments. ££

Stravaigin
28 Gibson Street, Hillhead; tel: 0141-334 2665; www.stravaigin.co.uk; daily breakfast, lunch and dinner.
Renowned for serving up the finest local ingredients with a laid-back vibe. Standouts include chargrilled Aberdeen Angus steak, Gressingham duck breast with black cherries, and a terrific range of cheeses. ££

Ubiquitous Chip
12 Ashton Lane; tel: 0141-334 5007; www.ubiquitouschip.co.uk; daily lunch and dinner.
The Chip is an institution in a converted mews stable. Enjoy fresh Scottish ingredients and a wonderful wine list amid stylish surroundings and playful artworks by Alasdair Gray. £££

The Wee Curry Shop
29 Ashton Lane; tel: 0141-357 5280; daily lunch and dinner.
Mother India's chain of curry shops offers a vast array of spicy offerings at reasonable prices. £

The sweeping view from Queen's Park over Glasgow and its glorious backdrop of hills.

Tour 8

South Side

Heading south of the Clyde, this 8-mile (13km), half-day tour takes in parks, grand old houses and arty attractions aplenty, from the Tramway to the Burrell Collection

This tour travels amid abandoned factories and red-bricked chimney stacks, the landmarks of Southside's post-industrial past. First stop is the old Copelawhill Tram Shed reborn as Tramway, a contemporary arts centre renowned for its fabulous visual and performance art shows, and its magical Hidden Gardens. Nearby Queen's Park offers magnificent views towards Loch Lomond and Lanark, while heading west, the wide green expanse of the Pollok Estate contains woodland walks, opportunities for mountain biking, and the late 18th-century period grandeur of Pollok House.

The famous Burrell Collection (closing for refurbishment 2016–19), home to priceless artworks, will be vastly improved with a £60-million overhaul, ensuring that 90 per cent of the collection with be on show. There are more uplifting delights at Rouken Glen and the walled, verdant oasis at Greenbank Garden, with its elegant Georgian mansion built by an 18th-century tobacco merchant. If you don't have the use of a bike,

Highlights

- Tramway
- Queen's Park
- Cycling and mountain biking in Pollok Country Park
- Burrell Collection
- Rouken Glen Park
- Greenbank Garden

Queen's Park Views

Queen's Park rises to an impressive summit, with panoramic views as far as Ben Lomond in the north and Lanark in the south. Near the main walkway is an oak tree planted by Belgian refugees after World War I and a beech tree planted in 1945 to commemorate the 20th anniversary of the founding of the United Nations.

a car would be the best means of transport for this tour, since it is not feasible on foot, and public transport is complicated.

HEADING SOUTH TO TRAMWAY

Start this walk from Argyle Street at Jamaica Street and, crossing Glasgow Bridge – built in 1899 following a Thomas Telford design – get in the middle lane, pass the Neoclassical tenements of **Carlton Place** to the left and head south along Eglinton Street. This area was a riverside hinterland for much of the 20th century and still bears the marks of commerce with warehouses, disused factories and railway arches.

On Albert Drive, the road leading to Pollockshields East railway station, is the fabulous **Tramway** ❶ arts centre (tel: 0845-330 3501; www.tramway.org; Tue–Fri noon–5pm, Sat–Sun noon–6pm; free) below a red-brick chimney stack. It is known for its compelling programme of visual and performance art, dance and experimental music. The Scottish Ballet is now based at Tramway too, in superb new studio facilities.

The majority of the art shows explore challenging, adult-orientated themes, which may not be suitable for children. This shouldn't dissuade families from visiting the centre, though, as one of Tramway's most popular attractions is its urban sanctuary, the Hidden Gardens, which sprouted from factory wasteland. Audioguides are available to help you identify the birdsong while you are walking around. Tramway'scafé-bar has views of the garden and is a great place to refuel and relax.

QUEEN'S PARK

Head east via Coplaw Street across to parallel Victoria Road, a wide avenue of small shops, pubs and restaurants, which leads to the gates of **Queen's Park** ❷. Although built in the reign of Victoria, and laid out by Sir Joseph Paxton of Crystal Palace fame, these rolling grounds take their name from Mary, Queen

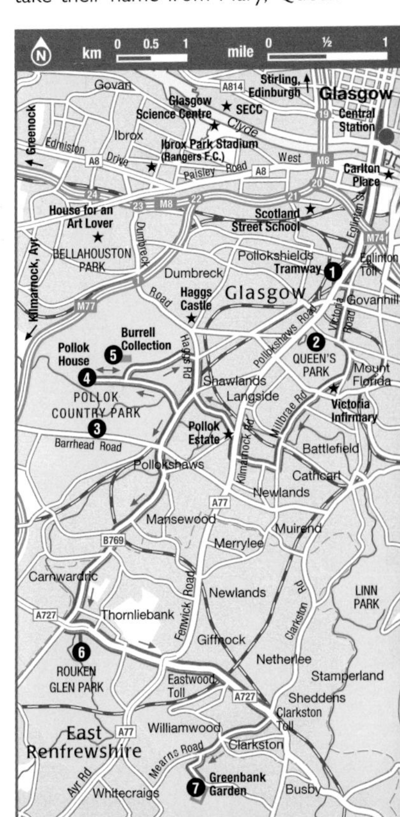

Pollok House mounts an impressive collection of Spanish art, in addition to works by William Blake.

of Scots, whose supporters lost the Battle of Langside nearby in 1568. The 148-acre (60-hectare) park occupies a commanding site, which was considerably enlarged in 1894 by the enclosure of the grounds of Camphill. It is a wonderful place for a picnic and has lots of amenities, should you be feeling more active, including five floodlit tennis courts, pitch and putt, bowling greens and a skateboard park. There is also a pond teeming with birdlife, including tufted ducks, moorhens, mallards, little grebe, coots and mute swans. The large boating pond provides serene moments during the summer months; there's also a café, which is open all year round.

The pond in Queen's Park.

TOWARDS POLLOK HOUSE AND COUNTRY PARK

Turning left at the gates, Langside Road, which is not signposted, runs round the park past the **Victoria Infirmary** – a huge hospital serving the whole of the south side of Glasgow – to the monument on Battle Place, designed by Alexander Skirving in 1887, and an imposing stone-cleaned former church, which has been converted to the *Church on the Hill* bar and restaurant.

Going straight ahead at the roundabout, follow Millbrae Road into Langside Drive, turn right at Newlands Road (you'll see a sign for Diarsie House School) and follow it to

Pollok Country Park is ideal for cyclists of all abilities.

Riverford Road. Go through the Pollokshaws area, once a thriving working-class heartland but now much demolished to make way for modern housing and a new railway line, and turn right onto Barrhead Road for the entrance to the Pollok Estate.

These beautifully sculpted grounds were given to the city as late as 1966 by Mrs Anne Maxwell Macdonald and now form **Pollok Country Park** ❸, where morning joggers and evening strollers enjoy the Highland cattle, heavy horses, art collections and woodland walks. The driveway runs past the Police Dog and Mounted Branch and parkland grazed by 'toffee-wrapper' cattle with their glowering fringes to **Pollok House** ❹ (tel: 0141-616 6410; www.nts.org.uk; daily 10am–5pm), a masterful William Adam construction dating from 1752. Its exquisite interior retains many original features and houses a fine collection of Spanish School paintings, and the gardens – including a particularly fine parterre and a full and productive walled garden – are bounded by a lazy curve of White Cart Water.

It has undergone a sympathetic restoration programme, and there is a good fully licensed restaurant in the kitchen. Pollok Country Park offers wonderful surroundings for cycling and is reached via Routes 7 and 75 of the National Cycle Network (www.sustrans.org.uk). You can also take your bicycle to Pollokshaws West station from Glasgow Central.

Mountain Biking

Pollok Country Park has three mountain-bike circuits suitable for different abilities. The **Green Circuit** offers a gentle ride; the **Blue Circuit** has steeper, more varied terrain and requires more skill; the **Red Circuit** is more akin to wild mountain topography and is not for the faint-hearted. Those seeking more two-wheeled thrills should head a few miles further south to **Cathkin Braes Country Park**, which was the venue of the Commonwealth Games 2014 Mountain Biking event.

Zip-wire fun in Pollok Country Park.

Sir William Burrell's incredible collection of artefacts from all over the world is on display at the famed Burrell Collection.

Medieval archways have been incorporated into the Burrell Collection's building.

BURRELL COLLECTION

Retracing the tour and forking left leads to the internationally famous **Burrell Collection** ❺ (www.glasgowlife.org.uk; the museum is subject to closure for restoration from 2016 to 2019, consult website for updates), the outstanding legacy of the shipping magnate Sir William Burrell, whose collector's instinct and eye for a bargain were on a par with his occasional rival, the American newspaper magnate William Randolph Hearst. He perfected the business method of selling his fleets of ships in a boom period and buying in a slump, and realised his considerable fortune in 1916 when he sold up to concentrate on his first love, art.

The collection is eclectic and idiosyncratic, with more than 9,000 objects from Egypt, Greece, the Middle East and South and East Asia, plus tapestries and stained glass from medieval Europe. Favourites with Glasgow visitors are the Degas collection, Rodin's *Thinker* (one of 14 casts made from the original) and the *Warwick Vase*, an 8-ton marble that dominates the courtyard. During closure parts of the collection will be displayed at Kelvingrove Art Gallery (see page 72).

In Glasgow City Council hands

Glasgow city received this fascinating collection in 1944 in a bequest of restrictive conditions, largely concerning Burrell's fears about the potential damage to his treasures from industrial air pollution. This meant that they lay in storage until 1983, when cleaner air and the acquisition of Pollok Estate allowed the construction of an award-winning building, which has deceptively simple lines and has drawn as much admiration as the museum's contents.

Medieval archways from the collection are blended with new red sandstone, and some halls have glass walls to the floor, giving the impression that the exhibits are being viewed in the open air. Others are completely enclosed and provide a warmly lit backdrop for some of the world's most exquisite tapestries. The collection also includes exhibits of entire rooms from Burrell's home at Hutton Castle in Berwickshire, and there's an excellent café-restaurant.

Stained glass at the Burrell Collection.

ROUKEN GLEN PARK

The road out of the park on the left – look for the carved woodpecker – leads onto Haggs Road. Turn right, get in the middle lane and follow it to Pollokshaws Road and the Round Toll roundabout, then take the B769 for Thornliebank. Stay on this road until the next roundabout and turn left onto the A727 for East Kilbride. Soon after joining the dual carriageway, take a right turn into Rouken Glen Park.

Rouken Glen Park ❻ was donated to the city by Mr A. Cameron

Rouken for Kids

There is plenty for children at Rouken Glen Park (www.roukenglenpark.co.uk), and it's all free. Two bouncy castles operate in the park (Mar–Oct weekends, public and school hols 11.30am–4.40pm). There are pony rides at 1.30pm in the summer and an outdoor gym and children's play area open year-round. The multi-sensory area and wheelchair-accessible play equipment were added in 2014, there's also a skate park for older kids, and a host of events are held here.

The collection offers several absorbing child-friendly activities.

Rouken Glen's natural waterfall was doubled in height in the early 1800s.

Corbett (later Lord Rowallan) in 1906 and passed to the adjoining Eastwood Council in 1984, after a dispute over running costs. Its loss to Glasgow was felt on an emotional level by many who remembered school trips to the large boating pond, where a motor launch would carry day-trippers round the islands, much to the indignation of nesting ducks.

Fears of the park's demise, however, were groundless, and a thriving range of commercial concerns – an attractive garden centre, art gallery and a signposted walkabout trail – have given it a new lease of life. The old attractions, however, remain unchanged: the waterfall tumbling into a mossy glen, the walled garden, a golf course and generous parkland.

GREENBANK GARDEN

Turning right at the exit, follow the A727 over Eastwood Toll rounda-

Exploring Greenbank Garden.

bout, through the suburbs of Clarkston to Clarkston Toll, where Greenbank Garden is signposted on the first right after the roundabout.

Greenbank Garden ❼ (www.nts.org.uk; garden: daily 9.30am–sunset; shop and tearoom: Nov–Mar Sat–Sun 1–4pm, Apr–Oct daily 11am–5pm; house: Apr–Oct Sun 2–4pm), which lies on Flenders Road, off Mearns Road, is a substantial walled garden, which many city dwellers regard as an oasis of calm. It is one of the few substantial properties the National Trust for Scotland has near the city. The gardens surround a tobacco merchant's 18th-century mansion; there are tours of the interior with its remarkable billiard room most Sunday afternoons. A tennis court has been converted into a garden for disabled visitors, with raised plant beds; the floral profusion encourages wildlife.

To return to the city, go to Clarkston Toll and follow the signs for the M77, taking junction 3 for the city centre.

The atmospheric walled Greenbank Garden is set around an 18th-century house.

Eating Out

The Boathouse
Rouken Glen Park; tel: 0141-638 6203; daily 8am–6pm.
This homely café located on the edge of Rouken Glen Park is very popular with families, who queue for the ice cream. Savoury options include panini, salads, pasta dishes and fish and chips. £

The Edwardian Kitchen Restaurant
Pollok House, Pollok Estate, 2060 Pollokshaws Road; tel: 0844-493 2202; daily 10am–5pm.
Amid the grand basement interiors of this award-winning restaurant, discerning diners are served a limited but excellent choice of mains including good veggie options. The home-baked cakes are legendary. £

Moyra Jane's
20 Kildrostan Street; tel: 0141-423 5628; Tue–Sat breakfast, lunch and dinner, Sun–Mon breakfast, lunch only.
This former bank building has marble-topped tables and wood-panelled walls – suitably solid surroundings for traditional, quality fare including lamb tagine, chicken stroganoff, vegetarian moussaka and massive meringues. £

Tramway Café-Bar
25 Albert Drive; tel: 0845-330 3501; Mon–Sat 9.30am–4.30pm and Sun noon–4pm.
An airy space looking onto the Hidden Gardens serving excellent, healthy vegetarian and vegan dishes, soups and sandwiches. £

Tea time at The Willow Tea Rooms.

Tour 9

Mackintosh Tour

Charles Rennie Mackintosh, pioneer of the Modern Movement, left the city of Glasgow a handsome artistic and architectural legacy, which never ceases to inspire

Rarely has a whole industry been founded on the designs of one architect, but Charles Rennie Mackintosh (1868–1928) was no ordinary architect. His vision and originality were at the forefront of the Modern Movement, and his imaginative buildings and clean, simple interior design were unique. Many of Mackintosh's buildings, however, were sadly neglected until the 1980s, but then his importance was realised and much-needed restoration of his works commenced. They lie spread across the city, making a comprehensive day tour moving from one gem to another is difficult, but the following guide highlights the most accessible and representative works.

The best source for information about Mackintosh himself, the history of the buildings and about access to Mackintosh properties as well as specialist tours is the **Charles Rennie Mackintosh Society** (tel: 0141-946 6600; www.crmsociety.com). They have an ongoing campaign to increase awareness of the architect and a push to have Mack-

Highlights

- The Lighthouse
- Glasgow School of Art
- The Mackintosh House
- Queen's Cross Church
- The Hill House
- House for an Art Lover
- Scotland Street School
- The Willow Tea Rooms

intosh buildings designated as Unesco World Heritage sites. The **Glasgow Visit Scotland Information Centre** (see page 123) is another valuable port of call. It's worthwhile buying a one-day Mackintosh Trail Ticket (£16), which allows visitors entry to all participating Mackintosh attractions and unlimited travel on the SPT subway and First bus services.

CITY-CENTRE SIGHTS

Starting in the city centre, **The Lighthouse** ❶ (tel: 0141-276 5365; www.thelighthouse.co.uk; Mon–Sat 10.30am–5pm, Sun noon–5pm, free; tours Sun–Wed 11am, booking required at least 24 hours in advance, Thu–Sat 11am, noon, 1pm, 2pm) features a Mackintosh Interpretation Centre to place the artist in his cultural context and help visitors find

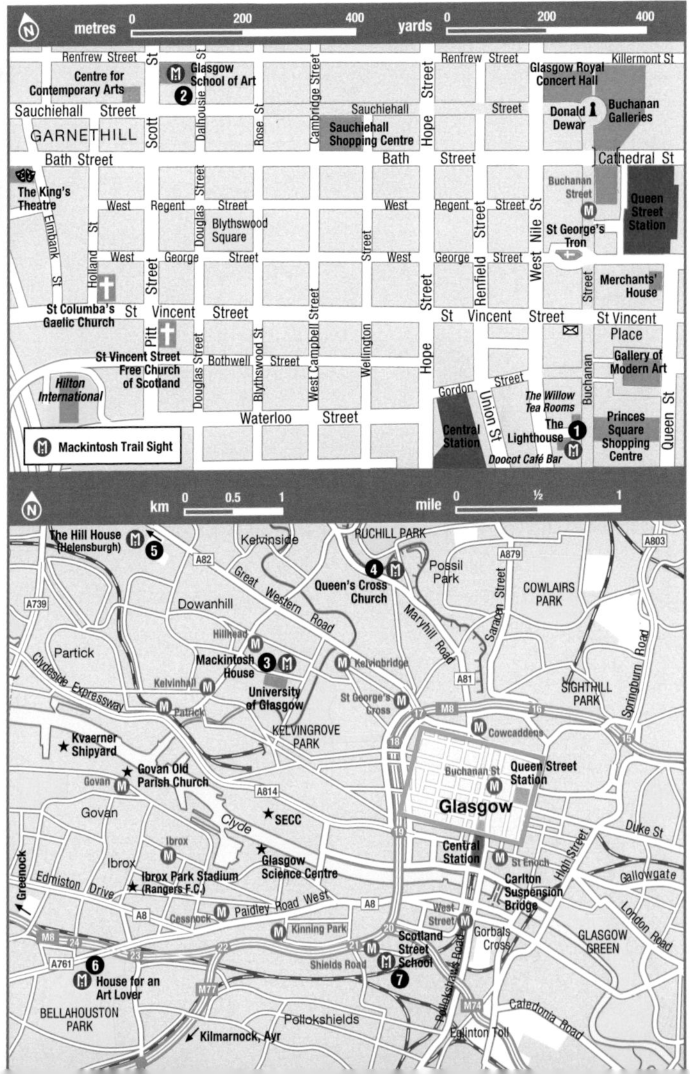

The staircase at The Lighthouse.

his buildings. Built to a design by Javier Mariscal, beside the tower of the old *Glasgow Herald* building in Mitchell Street, the rooftop platform offers close-up views of his work. It hosts a variety of temporary exhibitions exploring design and architectural themes and has a fabulous café/bar – the Doocot. In 2009, the Lighthouse Trust organisation – set up to champion Scottish architecture and design – found itself in financial trouble and went into administration. However Glasgow City Council stepped in to keep the centre open, and in 2012 it became Scotland's Centre for Design and Architecture.

GLASGOW SCHOOL OF ART

Along Sauchiehall Street and up Scott Street on the right is Mackintosh's crowning achievement, the **Glasgow School of Art** ❷ (www.gsa.ac.uk). Sadly this edifice, one of the most venerable art schools in the UK, with every stone, window and railing redolent of the architect's unique style, was the victim in May 2014 of a devastating fire, which ravaged the interior, in particular the iconic Mackintosh library.

Painstaking and meticulous restoration began in 2015, but it will take several years for the building to be returned to its former glory, both inside and out. However there are still opportunities for visitors to learn and see more of Mackintosh's work, despite being unable to gain access to the main building. In 2009 the ambitious, and sometimes controversial, Reid building (tours Sat 3pm) was approved, designed to complement the Mackintosh building opposite. It opened in 2014 with its state-of the-art A Window on Mackintosh Visitor Centre (tel: 0141-353 4526; daily 10am–4.30pm; free). Here, you can take the Mackintosh at

The Queen's Cross Church houses the Mackintosh Society HQ.

The Glasgow School of Art.

GSA Tour (daily 11am, 2pm, 3.15pm, also 11.30am July–mid-Sept, booking advised), a discovery of Mackintosh's life from student to master designer, led by award-winning student guides.

MACKINTOSH IN THE WEST END

In 1906, Mackintosh completely redesigned the interior of an ordinary terraced house at 78 Southpark Avenue for himself and his wife Margaret, whom he had married in 1900 just before being made a full partner at Honeyman & Keppie. They lived in it for eight years, and, before it was demolished in 1963, the fittings were removed and are now on display as the **Mackintosh House** ❸ (charge) in the **Hunterian Gallery** (see page 81; Tue–Sat 10am–5pm, Sun 11am–4pm), which is a brief taxi ride from the School of Art.

Another short taxi hop away from here is Garscube Road's **Queen's Cross Church** ❹, which is now the headquarters of the **Charles Rennie Mackintosh Society** and is open to visitors. After admiring the red-sandstone exterior with its unusual blocky turrets, dip your head inside to marvel at the interiors. The blue stained-glass window designs play on the Gothic style to startling effect, while the handsome relief carving on wood and stonework complements the feeling of sparseness, light and space. As well as being the best place for finding out about Mackintosh events and tours, the Mackintosh Church at Queen's Cross has a superb library. The shop stocks an extensive range of Mackintosh books and objects based on the great man's designs.

Rennie Mac's Early Years

One of 13 children of a police superintendent, Mackintosh was born in Parsons Street, where he would later create the Martyrs' School. He attended night classes at Glasgow's School of Art – then in the McLellan Galleries – before joining Honeyman & Keppie, for whom he did his best work. His first major public building, the former *Glasgow Herald* office – renamed The Lighthouse in a design by Barcelona Olympics maestro Javier Mariscal – was the focal point of Glasgow's year as City of Architecture in 1999.

Glasgow's architectural hero, Charles Rennie Mackintosh.

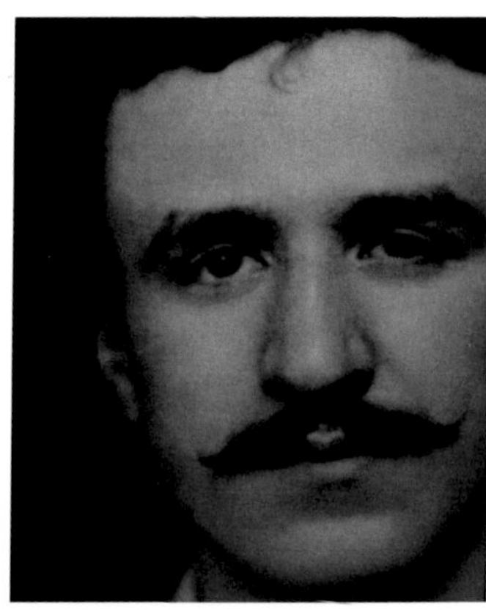

The Hill House, set in attractive gardens.

THE HILL HOUSE AT HELENSBURGH

The Hill House ❺ (tel: 01436-673 900; www.nts.org.uk; Apr–Oct 11.30am–5.30pm) is not in Glasgow, but it should be included in any tour of Mackintosh works. A 40-minute train ride away in Helensburgh (Scotrail; tel: 0344-811 0141), it's by far the most attractive of his domestic commissions. Built on a commanding site for the publisher Walter Blackie, the fittings have been meticulously conserved by the National Trust for Scotland.

Back to School

Children and adults will enjoy a look around Scotland Street School's three classroom reconstructions, which show the changing face of teaching and childhood from the Victorian era through World War II to the classroom of the 1950s and 1960s. Particularly evocative are the barrel-vaulted cookery room, cloakrooms and ceramic-tiled drill hall, which have been restored to Mackintosh's original 1906 designs.

SOUTHSIDE MASTERPIECES

House for an Art Lover ❻ (www.houseforanartlover.co.uk; tel: 0141-353 4770; times vary owing to private events so check before visiting) was created from a portfolio that Mackintosh presented for a design competition in 1901. Following his drawings, the house was built in a beautiful parkland setting beside the Victorian walled garden in Bellahouston Park, and contains striking details and interiors, plus a café and shop (both

A classroom reconstruction at Scotland Street School.

daily 10am–5pm). The nearest underground station is Ibrox; nearest mainline station is Dumbreck. The house is about 15 minutes by taxi from the city centre.

Scotland Street School ❼ (tel: 0141-287 0500; www.glasgowlife.org.uk; Tue–Thu and Sat 10am–5pm, Fri and Sun 11am–5pm; free) is most easily reached by underground. Get off at Shields Road station, and the school's twin towers of leaded glass and red sandstone are clearly visible across the road.

Built between 1903 and 1906, the school is clearly Glasgow-style and offers a fascinating look at developments in Scottish education. There are interactive displays, which explore the school world and design tools to see if you can match the master draughtsman Mackintosh. Even more fascinating are the accounts of former pupils' recollections of their school days. The archive follows the decades, detailing the minutiae of childhood and background events in Scottish and world history. Themes covered include classroom discipline, school trips, school attire, evacuation and World War II, playground antics and the changing local environment. Two live interpretation sessions, Horrible Heidie and Time Travellers – School Days, allow children to experience the classes of yesteryear.

Inside the elegant House for an Art Lover.

Eating Out

Art Lovers Café

House for an Art Lover, Bellahouston Park; tel: 0141-353 4770; daily 10am–5pm.

Set within one of Mackintosh's finest houses, this popular café is open to people visiting the house and those who simply want to come and eat. The elegant surroundings embody Mackintosh's design ideals, and the dishes are presented with style and skill. The menu places huge emphasis on seasonal produce, so it changes regularly, but you may find sea bream, Aberdeen beef or roast rump of lamb at any given time. In summer there is a lovely outdoor seating area. £

The Willow Tea Rooms

97 Buchanan Street; tel: 0141-204 5242; www.willowtearooms.co.uk; Mon–Sat 9am–5pm, Sun 10.30am–5pm.

This is a faithful re-creation of the innovative design work Mackintosh carried out for well-known restaurateur Kate Cranston at the turn of the 20th century. The originals of the White Room and the Blue Room are in the care of Glasgow City Council. More Mackintosh interiors, afternoon tea and scones can be enjoyed at the other Willow Tea Rooms located at 217 Sauchiehall Street (tel: 0141-332 0521). £

The Sir Walter Scott steamer plies the waters of Lock Katrine.

Tour 10

Excursion to Loch Lomond

An 80-mile (130km) foray into the Highlands, Loch Lomond and the Trossachs National Park, dipping into Britain's largest lake and visiting beguiling villages

You tak' the High Road,
and I'll tak' the Low Road,
and I'll be in Scotland afore ye.

The words of the Loch Lomond song distil the romance of the glens for Scots the world over, but for the most part, the reality of the High Road these days is a wide dual carriageway. Following signs for Crianlarich, the A82 continues westwards from Great Western Road in the centre of Glasgow along the north bank of the Clyde past Bowling, Dumbarton – the ancient capital of Strathclyde, with its castle on the rock – and Balloch.

This is a long excursion, but once you are at the loch, the roads mellow out, and the countryside ranges from the lush and rolling to true Highland drama. The route includes points at which you have to double back on yourself, but not for more than a few miles.

Highlights

- Balloch
- Drymen
- Balmaha
- Priory of Inchmahome
- Aberfoyle
- Loch Katrine

LUSS, ON THE BANKS OF LOCH LOMOND

Following the Crianlarich signs, head first for the village of **Luss** ❶. Although surrounded on the outskirts by tourist services, the rose-clad cottages and the old pier are attractive. On the

Setting off on the West Highland Way.

other side of the main carriageway, a farm road signposted for Glen Luss runs up to some of the best hill-walking within easy reach of the city. A series of Corbetts (Scottish hills ranging between 2,500ft/762m and 3,000ft/914m) afford spectacular views to the Clyde estuary and the western islands. The weather in the mountains can change quickly, so always carry a map and dress warmly.

BALLOCH, DRYMEN AND BALMAHA

Returning south, turn left at the roundabout signed for **Balloch** ❷ and left at the next roundabout. This leads into the heart of Loch Lomond's only town of any size. It hosts **Loch Lomond Shores** (tel: 01389-751 031; www.lochlomondshores.com; free), a visitor centre with shops, café and innovative aquarium (Sea Life; tel: 01389-721 500) complete with sharks and a giant sea turtle . Boats of all shapes and sizes crowd the banks and pontoons, as the loch empties into the River Leven on its way to the Clyde.

The A811, signposted for Drymen, wanders through undulating farmland, passing only one village of note, **Gartocharn** ❸. The small hill at the back is called **Duncryne** and is worth the gentle climb for views of the water meadows of the southern loch, the wooded islands and the higher hills in the distance, including Ben Lomond.

At the junction with the A809, turn left to **Drymen** ❹, a delightful village 11 miles (18km) north of Glasgow. It retains a charming rural atmosphere. The cosy **Clachan Inn** (tel: 01360-660 824), established in 1734, is a good place to eat or enjoy a wee dram.

West Highland Way

The West Highland Way, a 96-mile (154km) walk from Milngavie, on the outskirts of Glasgow, to Fort William, starts at a granite obelisk in Douglas Street. The route follows ancient communication tracks as well as drove roads, military roads and disused railway tracks. The first 5-mile (8km) stage to Carbeth involves 500ft (148m) of ascent – a tame but enjoyable preamble to later challenges including climbing the Devil's Staircase below Glencoe's jagged Aonach Eagach ridge. See also www.west-highland-way.co.uk.

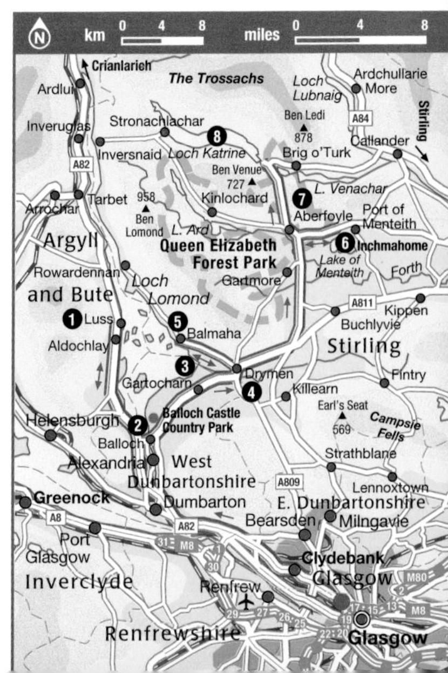

Balmaha's boatyard is the place to pick up a loch cruiser.

The B837 from the centre runs 5 miles (8km) to **Balmaha ❺**, a village lying on the Highland Boundary Fault, separating the Highlands from the Lowlands. A scatter of whitewashed houses surrounds the small inlet where **Balmaha's boatyard** (tel: 01360-870 214) caters for fishermen and loch cruisers, and offers places on the regular mailboat round the islands in summer – an unusual day trip. The **Oak Tree Inn** (tel: 01360-870 357) is a good place to eat or stay. A path leads from the car park to Conic Hill; from the summit it is possible to see the 37 islands in the loch.

The historic Priory of Inchmahome.

LAKE OF MENTEITH

Returning to Drymen, the A811 meanders north and east before joining the A81 north across the flatlands towards the hills of the Queen Elizabeth Forest. At the Rob Roy Hotel, the route goes left to Aberfoyle, but turning right along the A81 for a short distance to the B8034 brings you to the island priory of **Inchmahome ❻** (Apr–Sept daily 10am–4.15am, Oct daily 10am–3.15pm; charge includes ferry) on the Lake of Menteith, the only 'lake' in Scotland. These beautiful 12th-century Augustinian remains once sheltered Mary, Queen of Scots.

ABERFOYLE

Follow the A821 for the Trossachs. You'll next hit **Aberfoyle ❼**, a tourist honeypot. The road north negotiates a startling series of hairpins as it climbs past the **David Marshall Lodge** to Duke's Pass then descends to Loch Achray. One of the small

Boats moored at Loch Katrine.

peaks on the far side of the loch is **Ben A'an** which affords a superb vista of Loch Katrine, Sir Walter Scott's inspiration for *The Lady of the Lake* (1810).

Before Ben A'an, the main road branches off to **Loch Katrine 8**, where the steam yacht *Sir Walter Scott* sails on Glasgow's water supply (www.lochkatrine.com; Apr–Oct; call to check times; tel: 01877-376 315/6). Bikes are available to hire for a ride along the loch road. For the quickest way back to Glasgow, travel 10 miles (16km) to Callander, then on to Stirling to join the M9.

Eating Out

Balloch

Balloch House

Balloch Road; tel: 01389-752 579; daily lunch and dinner.
Serves hearty fish and chips alongside more adventurous dishes. £

Near Balloch

Cameron House Hotel

A82; tel: 01389-755 565; www.qhotels.co.uk; Cameron Grill: Mon–Sat breakfast and dinner, Sun lunch only; Martin Wishart's: Wed dinner only, Thu–Sun lunch and dinner.
This luxurious lochside former stately home offers several dining options including Martin Wishart's Michelin-starred eatery, which serves delicious dishes such as turbot with oyster, squid and baby leeks. £–£££

Duck Bay Marina

A82; tel: 01389-751 234; www.duckbay.co.uk; daily breakfast, lunch and dinner.
This modern hotel has large picture windows with glorious loch views. Expect classics such as haggis, plus pasta dishes and crêpes. ££

Loch Lomond

Everyone has heard of it, but the loch aspect of Loch Lomond is just one of the shimmering jewels in what is Scotland's most famous and diversified national park

OUTDOOR TREATS

Loch Lomond and the Trossachs National Park (www.lochlomond-trossachs.org; visitor centre in Balmaha) stretches a little west of the loch, north to Tyndrum, east to Callander and south to Balloch. Straddling the West Highland fault line, the heather-clad hills abound with 'darksome glens and gleaming lochs', as wrote legendary Scottish author Sir Walter Scott.

This area is a magnet for walkers, cyclists and those who love water sports. The main information centre in Balloch is run by VisitScotland (www.visitscotland.com) and has every kind of information about the park, including geological history, walking routes, cycle paths and details about all the guides and companies who provide tours, mountain-bike excursions, horse riding, fishing and boat trips on the lochs (notably the *Sir Walter Scott* steamer on Loch Katrine; see page 103).

WALKING COUNTRY

There are a multitude of easy and short walks, such as the **Creag an Tuirc** walk, which begins at Balquidder (2.5 miles/4km, about 2 hours), and the hillier Cruach Tairbeirt walk (4.7 miles/7.5km, about 3 hours), taking you up to 1,485ft (450m). In exchange for your efforts you receive glorious

The Loch Lomond park is perfect walking country.

Flora and Fauna

As you travel away from the sparkling shores of the loch, you're greeted by spectacular hills, glens with densely wooded forests and a real sense that you're surrounded by the wild. The national park boasts 200 species of birds, including buzzards, ospreys, golden eagles, peregrine falcons, pied flycatchers, black grouse and capercaillies – although you're more likely to hear the cricking noise of these than see them among the heathery thickets. The park is home to 25 percent of Britain's wild plant species: there are 500 flowering species and ferns, with rarities such as wood anemone, wood sorrel and, magnificent in May, thick blankets of bluebells. As for fauna, take your time and keep quiet and you have some chance of being in the presence of – if not seeing – red deer, polecats, pine martens and wildcats. Meanwhile, Loch Lomond is the largest freshwater loch in the UK; within it swim salmon, pike and powan, a whitefish only found in one other place.

views of Loch Lomond – weather permitting.

If you must climb a hill, try **Ben Ledi**, classified as a Corbett, a smaller set of Scottish hills (6.25 miles 10km, 4–6 hours). It might be wee but on a clear day you can see the Firth of Forth from the summit at 2,883ft (879m). For those craving to bag a Munro, Scotland's highest peaks, 3,707ft (1,130m) -high **Ben Lui** (13 miles/21km, about 7 hours) is a must-climb. For much of the year its Coire Gaothaich (Windy Corrie) is filled with snow, lending it an alpine character. Ben Lui is reached from Tyndrum.

For those with time, the inclination and broken-in boots, the famous **West Highland Way** (96miles/154km, up to 1,850ft/550m) from Milngavie to Fort William is one of the most trampled and loved walks in Scotland. It takes between 7 and 10 days.

Whatever walk you choose to do, be prepared for a dramatic change in the weather, even in the warmest months, and have proper footwear, a map and compass (the ability to use these properly is a must too!) as well as waterproof clothing. Also, leave word of your plans with your accommodation.

The picturesque Chatelherault Country Park.

Tour 11

Excursion to Clyde Valley

Two country parks, riverside walks, the David Livingstone Centre, Craignethan Castle and fascinating New Lanark make this a stimulating jaunt

Highlights

- Strathclyde Country Park
- Duke of Hamilton's Mausoleum
- David Livingstone Centre
- Chatelherault Country Park
- Craignethan Castle
- Lanark
- New Lanark

The River Clyde, the wonderful Clyde,
The name of it thrills me and fills me with pride.

When Glaswegians sing praise of the river that gave their city meaning, they think of the clatter of shipyards and the sway of giant cranes. But further down the valley is an altogether different river, wandering through gentle hills and watering fertile orchards and fruit farms. This 45-mile (72km) tour requires a car, or a bike for the very fit, taking in country parks, lots of intriguing history and a Unesco World Heritage Site at New Lanark.

STRATHCLYDE COUNTRY PARK

The M8 snakes through the centre of Glasgow, and it is possible to join it at many points. Once on the eastbound carriageway, follow signs for Carlisle and Edinburgh through the industrial eastern suburbs until you reach junction 8 with the M73, then follow signs for Carlisle.

Off the A723 between a cluster of Glasgow's satellite towns – including **Hamilton** and **Motherwell** – is

The Chatelherault Country Park is packed with bucolic charm.

Strathclyde Country Park ❶. It's accessible via junction 5 of the M74. This huge recreation area includes a man-made loch that offers sailing, windsurfing and water-skiing, along with an amusement park, **M&D's** (tel: 01698-333 777; www.scotlandsthemepark.com), featuring some of the biggest rides in Scotland.

The **Low Parks Museum** (tel: 01698-452 382; Mon–Sat 10am–5pm, Sun noon–5pm; free), built on the site of the Hamilton Palace, complete with a mezzanine café, is located on Muir Street. It tells the turbulent history of the town, its regiment – the Cameronians – and the Hamilton family, whose spectacular **Mausoleum** ❷, built by the 10th Duke in the 1840s, has impassive stone lions guarding the enormous bronze doors and beautiful marblework within.

DAVID LIVINGSTONE CENTRE

A few miles up the A724 at Blantyre is the **David Livingstone Centre** ❸ (tel: 0844-493 2207; www.nts.org.uk; Apr–Dec daily 11am–5pm), a memorial to Scotland's greatest missionary explorer, who was born here in 1813. Brought up as a poor factory boy, he led an eventful life, which included the discovery of the Victoria Falls on the border between Zambia and Zimbabwe while on a journey across the African continent in 1855. He died of dysentery in 1873 while searching for the then-unknown source of the River Nile.

CHATELHERAULT COUNTRY PARK

Returning through Hamilton, join the A72 for Lanark and, as the suburbs give way to countryside, the gates of **Chatelherault Country Park** ❹ (tel: 01698-426 213; visitor centre: daily 10am–5pm; West Lodge: Sun–Thu 10am–4.30pm; free) open up on the right. The visitor centre, once the kennels for the hunting dogs of the Duke of Hamilton, butts onto the main building, designed by William Adam for the Fifth Duke and completed in 1744. The building fell into dereliction – mining subsidence has added a jaunty slope to some floors – but a masterful restoration was completed in 1987 allowing visitors to fully appreciate the superb plasterwork with its ornate figures from Classical mythology.

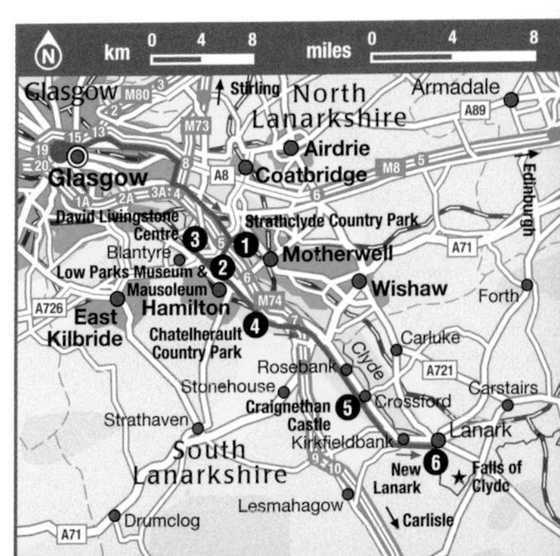

The fascinating New Lanark is a Unesco World Heritage Site.

CRAIGNETHAN CASTLE

The A72 now follows the twists and turns of the Clyde as it runs through a valley of soft-fruit, tomato and vegetable growers, past Dalserf's 1655 church and the pretty half-timbered village of Rosebank with its Popinjay Hotel and Spa (tel: 01555-860 441). Slightly further on, a sign points right to **Craignethan Castle** ❺ (tel: 01555-860 364; Apr–Sept daily 9.30am–5.30pm), a sombre keep situated 2 miles (3km) up a narrow and twisting road. Dating back to around 1530, this rambling ruin was one of the last great family tower fortresses, and from it the Hamilton family played a pivotal role in Scottish politics, including supporting Mary, Queen of Scots, whom they sheltered here after her abdication in 1567.

Although Sir Walter Scott denied that its ivy-clad ruins were the inspiration for Tillietudlem Castle in the Waverley novel *Old Mortality* – and

Riverside Walks

Chatelherault Country Park consists of nearly 500 acres (200 hectares) of the Avon Gorge, one of the least polluted of the Clyde's tributaries. There are miles of riverside walks and picturesque sights here, including the dramatic Duke's Bridge, the medieval mystery of Cadzow Castle and rolling parkland featuring white cattle, whose lineage dates back to Roman times.

The Hamilton Mausoleum.

indeed he is said to have considered settling here instead of Abbotsford – its remote location and air of mystery are resonant for many of Claverhouse and the Covenanting bands.

LANARK AND NEW LANARK

Back on the A72, the road continues through Kirkfieldbank to the historic town of **Lanark**, a slope trodden during the Wars of Independence (1286–1328) by the raggle-taggle hordes of William Wallace, whose statue looks down from an 18th-century church along a bustling main street divided by pretty floral displays. This busy market town was founded in 1140 by King David. He established a castle here, long since disappeared.

As you follow the signs at the top of the street for New Lanark, the road twists down again to the Clyde and one of the most remarkable episodes in Scotland's industrial history, as well as one of its most adventurous heritage restoration projects. At first sight, **New Lanark** ❻ (tel: 01555-661 345; www.newlanark.org; Apr–Oct 10am–5pm, Nov–Mar 10am–4pm) seems little more than a group of stone-built warehouses, but it was here that David Dale and his son-in-law Robert Owen conducted a social experiment that was to have lasting repercussions for the bitterly oppressed working classes.

Dale, from Stewarton, made his fortune in weaving and French yarns. In 1785, using the abundant water power of the Clyde, he set up the New Lanark Mills, which, at their height, employed over 2,000 workers, many of them children. Along with Owen, who assumed management in 1799, he introduced a regime of decent housing, reasonable wages, education and healthcare, to prove his theory that contented workers were productive workers. His message did

The old looms at New Lanark.

as much to create a social revolution as the mills had done for industry, and, as a result, workers' rights began to be considered seriously elsewhere.

The village, now a Unesco World Heritage Site, has been restored as a living community complete with hotel and shops, and the millworkers' tenement rows are desirable properties. There is also a youth hostel here (tel: 01555-666 710). In the Visitor Centre, various audiovisual rides show life in the mill past, present and future.

Along the river, a sylvan walk leads to the **Falls of Clyde**, where the Scottish Wildlife Trust organises badger watches, and the keen-eyed may spot kingfishers, owls and pipistrelle bats, as night descends.

Eating Out

Hamilton

Di Maggio's

42 Gateside Street; tel: 01698-891 828; www.dimaggios.co.uk; daily lunch and dinner.

Child-friendly Italian restaurant serving decent pizzas and pastas, American diner classics, and decadent *dolci* treats such as raspberry ripple cheesecake. £

Inside the mind of the poet at Robert Burns Birthplace Museum.

Tour 12

Excursion to Burns Country

On the trail of poet Robert Burns, visiting the haunts of Scotland's national bard, including the Bachelors' Club and Burns Cottage, his birthplace

For a' that, an' a' that,
It's coming yet for a' that,
That Man to Man, the world o'er,
Shall brothers be for a' that

Scots, with their tradition of struggle for social justice, embrace the egalitarian theme that runs through the works of their National Bard, Robert 'Rabbie' Burns (1759–96). The memory of his turbulent life is kept alive at Burns Suppers across the world at the end of January. Burns's associations with Glasgow were tenuous – minor dealings with publishers – but the literary legacy he left and the memorials to his origins in Burns Country are easily accessible from the city. A car is required for this excursion to the southwest coast taking in the various Burns-related monuments and sights.

Highlights

- Burns House Museum, Mauchline
- Highland Mary Monument
- Bachelors' Club
- Ayr
- Burns National Heritage Park
- Burns Cottage
- Auld Alloway Kirk
- Brig O'Doon
- Souter Johnnie's Cottage

MAUCHLINE AND FAILFORD

Leave the city on the M8 westbound and join the M77, then the A77 towards Ayr. Turn off just after Kilmarnock on to the A76 (signposted Dumfries). This road leads through typical

The red-bricked Burns House Museum.

Ayrshire countryside to the village of Mauchline, on the outskirts of which stands the Scots baronial folly of the **National Burns Memorial Tower**, established in 1896. The **Burns House Museum** ❶ (tel: 01387-255 297; Tue–Sat 10am–4pm; free), in which the poet lived, is in the village centre, as is **Poosie Nansie's Tavern**, said to have inspired part of *The Jolly Beggars*.

Leaving the village on the B743, the road winds towards **Failford** ❷, a scatter of houses in a small dip. A path behind a sign to Failford Gorge – easy to miss – leads to a monument to **Highland Mary**, the mysterious but beautiful woman for whom Burns wrote *My Highland Lassie O*. This is one of the lesser Burns monuments, but the inscription on the pillar is touching:

That sacred hour can I forget,
Can I forget the hallowed grove,
Where by the winding Ayr we met,
To live one day of parting love.

BACHELORS' CLUB

Past Failford, a brief diversion on the right leads to Tarbolton, where the National Trust for Scotland is the custodian of the **Bachelors' Club** ❸ (tel: 0844-493 2146; www.nts.org.uk; Apr–Sept Fri–Tue 1–5pm, last admission 4.30pm; morning visits available for pre-booked groups). The 17th-century thatched house just off the main road is where the poet and his cronies formed a debating club with easy access to the inn next door. It was here that Burns was introduced to the Freemasonry that shaped his philosophy of the brotherhood of Man.

Returning to the B743, it is 6 miles (10km) to **Ayr** ❹, a resort town with sandy beaches and a statue of Burns in the main square. Crossing the main road over the River Ayr, the 15th-century pedestrian bridge

The spooky graveyard at Auld Alloway Kirk.

on the left is the **Auld Brig** and the pillared steeple straight ahead is Ayr Town Hall. Burns was baptised in the Auld Kirk.

ROBERT BURNS BIRTHPLACE MUSEUM

Heading out of town on the A719 (signposted for Maidens), look for a sign for the Heads of Ayr then turn left at the first sign for **Alloway**, a pretty village of rose-entwined cottages that is at the heart of Burns Country. A car park on the left at the junction with the B7024 to Maybole serves the **Burns National Heritage Park**, which includes **Burns Cottage**, the poet's birthplace, and the **Robert Burns Birthplace Museum** ❺ (tel: 0844-493 2601; www.burnsmuseum.org.uk; Apr–Sept daily 10am–5.30pm, Oct–Mar daily 10am–5pm). His birthplace is a clay-wall-and-thatch house, which the poet's father William built and where he instilled young Robert's love of language and learning. The museum contains the most important collection of Burns's work, including the original copy of the *Kilmarnock Edition*, the first collection of poems he published to raise cash in order to emigrate to Jamaica. The state-of-the-art technology aims to bring the life, loves and demons of the poet to life. The museum holds more than 5,5000 manuscripts, books, personal artefacts and artworks relating to Burns and his legacy. As well as these permanent collections there are temporary exhibitions on Burns-related art, and poetry readings and musical events. There are also tours of the site with expert guides to tell the history of Burns and the area.

Burns by Bike

Friendly Cycle Ayrshire (tel: 01290-550 276; www.cycleayrshire.co.uk) organises a wide range of rides throughout the county, led by expert riders over mainly minor roads. Various excursions cater for all abilities, including beginners, returners to cycling and families, including the occasional Burns by Bike tour. The more taxing 30-mile (48km) circular ride starts at Rozelle Park in Ayr. A decent level of fitness is suggested for this ride.

Auld Alloway Kirk, also in the complex but just a little further on, is a 16th-century refuge that was a ruin even in Burns's day and was last used in 1756. Its gloomy graveyard holds the remains of Burns's father, and the mossy crypts and worn stones with their goblin carvings are a suitably chilling setting for the dance of the witches as the Devil – *'a tousie tyke, black, grim and large'* – played the pipes and *'gart them skirl'*.

When Tam, inspired by John Barleycorn, interrupted their dance with the shout: *'Weel done, Cutty Sark'*, his mare Meg fled to **Brig O'Doon** nearby to escape minus *'her ain grey tail'*. This 13th-century cobbled bridge with its ancient arch now stands below the **Burns Monument**, a Grecian tower designed by Thomas Hamilton and opened in 1823.

TOWARDS SOUTH AYRSHIRE

The B7024 carries on to **Maybole**, where Burns's father and mother met in 1756. Joining the A77, signposted for Stranraer, the road leads past the 13th-century ruins of **Crossraguel Abbey** ❻ with its abbot's tower and dovecote, to the village of Kirkoswald. Here the National Trust for Scotland maintains the thatched **Souter Johnnie's Cottage** ❼ (tel: 01655-760 603; www.nts.org.uk; Apr–Sept Fri–Tue 11.30am–5pm), a representation of the daily life of the cobbler who was the inspiration behind Tam O'Shanter's *'ancient, trusty, drouthy crony'*.

This is a long but fascinating run. Finish with drinks at the **Trump Turnberry Resort Hotel** (tel: 01655-331 000), scene of so many memorable moments in Open golf history.

Eating Out

Ayr

The Waterfront

4 South Harbour Street; tel: 01292-280 212; www.waterfront-ayr.co.uk; daily 10am–9pm (until 10pm Fri–Sat).

This stylish restaurant overlooking the river serves a wide range of well-cooked dishes from fillet steak to mussels, plus coffee, homemade cakes and cocktails. £

Burns Cottage, the birthplace of the beloved Scottish bard.

Helpful signs in Aberfoyle.

HANDCRAFTS
& GIFTS
01877 389302
Chill Out
HOLISTIC
THERAPIES
01877 389302
POST OFFICE
CSS

Natural splendours await for those keen to get active.

Travel Tips

Active Pursuits

For all its municipal grandeur and urban chic, this 'dear green place' is surrounded by hills and water and full of things to do.

Walkers are less than an hour away from the splendours of Loch Lomond and the Trossachs National Park (see page 104), which has Munros, Corbetts, heather hill rambles, forest walks and nature trails that will allow you to glimpse some of the 500 species of flowering plant and 250 species of bird that reside here. For the really serious outdoors enthusiast, there's the West Highland Way to explore, which takes about five to seven days to walk. It takes you from Milngavie, just north of Glasgow, to Fort William, a distance of 96 miles (154km), passing through some of Scotland's most stunning scenery. For information on all the walks that can be done in this area, visit www.lochlomond-trossachs.org.

BOATING

Glasgow is a city built on its maritime might, and many marinas and boat clubs line the waterways. Sail out of the Firth of Clyde and head north along the shores and you will

Cycling in the Clyde Valley.

be astounded by the beauty of the sea lochs, rocky outcrops and inlets, not to mention the isles of Islay and Mull. Experienced sailors should visit www.sailscotland.co.uk for information on all the routes, charts, sites, nature and companies that offer boats for hire. For those who can't sail but want to go out on the open waves, the *Waverley* (www.waverley excursions.co.uk) is the last remaining seagoing paddle steamer in the world and does summer sails along the Clyde, as well as to the northern lochs and nearby islands of Arran, Bute and Cumbrae.

Boating is popular.

CYCLING

There are lots of cycle paths around Glasgow and along the Clyde. Within the city, the Glasgow Mountain Bike Circuit in Pollok Park has a green circuit for those wanting a gentle ride through the woods, a blue circuit for a bit of bounce and climb, and a red circuit for those who want really rugged terrain. You can rent a bike from www.nextbike.co.uk/en/glasgow.

FISHING

One benefit of the demise of heavy industry is that the Clyde is less polluted now, and trout and salmon have returned. Angling is becoming increasingly popular on the banks of the rivers of Glasgow. The United Clyde Angling Protective Association Ltd (www.ucapaltd.com) looks after the Clyde and its tributaries, and you can buy a permit from Anglers Attic (tel: 01698-359 757) to fish on a particular stretch.

Football's Old Firm

Football fans will associate Glasgow with its two big teams, Celtic and Rangers. The rivalry between the Old Firm (as they are collectively known) is embedded in the history of the city, and passions are as fiery as ever – joint initiatives to confront its nastier side continue. Celtic Park, otherwise known as Parkhead (or Paradise), is in the East End (www.celticfc.co.uk), while Rangers, who were forced into the the lower ranks of the SPFL after going into administration, make their home at Ibrox in the Southside (www.rangers.co.uk). Both clubs offer stadium tours.

Old Firm clashes are notorious for their intensity.

Playing a few holes at the Pollok Golf Club, with the impressive Pollok House in the background.

GOLF

There are dozens of golf courses in and around Glasgow. Douglas Park (tel: 0141-942 0985; www.douglasparkgolfclub.co.uk) is an attractive 18-hole course north of the city near Milngavie. Lethamhill (tel: 0141-276 0810; junction 8 off the M8) is a municipal 18-hole course overlooking Hogganfield Loch.

HORSE RIDING

There are a few horse-riding centres around the outskirts of Glasgow. Easterton Stables in Milngavie (www.eastertonstables.co.uk) offers lessons, or, if you can already handle a horse, you can hack along the dips and dells of Mugdock Country Park in the Campsie Fells, surely one of the most delightful ways to see the scenery.

A falconry demonstration at Kelburne Country Park.

Children's Activities

Glasgow is a city with activities for all ages. At **Hampden Park** (tel: 0141-616 6139; www.scottishfootballmuseum.org.uk; Mon–Sat 10am–5pm, Sun 11am–5pm), Scotland's national football stadium, kids and adults alike will enjoy the Scottish Football Hall of Fame, and have an opportunity to tour the stadium.

Kelburn Castle & Estate, which is located near Largs (tel: 01475-568 685; www.kelburnestate.com), boasts waterfalls, an assault course and 'The Secret Forest'. The refurbished **Summerlee Museum of Scottish Industrial Life** at Coatbridge (tel: 01236-638 460) offers kids the chance to ride on an old tram as part of Scotland's only electric-driven tramway. Also out this way, the **Time Capsule** (tel: 01236-449 572; www.thetimecapsule.info), with swimming and ice-skating among volcanoes and cavemen, is worth a visit.

Themed Holidays

Whether you have a day, a weekend or a week, Glasgow is full of opportunities to learn a new skill or to do something useful.

ARTISTIC BREAKS

Although the devastating fire of 2014 has rendered the Mackintosh building at the **Glasgow School of Art** (tel: 0141-353 4500; www.gsa.ac.uk) off limits during restoration, a wide range of short art-related courses are still being run by the school in July and August. This allows you to learn and work alongside resident lecturers and guest artists located in a number of the studios across the campus. You can also book cheap accommodation within the student halls of residence, with en-suite accommodation at Margaret Macdonald House (run as Glasgow Metro in July and August by the Scottish Youth Hostelling Association, or SYHA, www.syha.org.uk.

BAGPIPING

If you've ever dreamed of mastering the bagpipes, you can learn to pipe at the **College of Piping** (tel: 0141-334-3587; www.college-of-piping.co.uk). Evening, day and week-long courses at hugely attractive prices are available during term times throughout the year.

BUDDHIST RETREATS

If you feel the need for inner peace, you have a good chance of finding it at **Kagyu Samye Ling** (tel: 01387-373 232; www.samyeling.org), Europe's oldest Tibetan Buddhist monastery. A range of retreats and courses cover all aspects of the practice. The monastery is a two-hour drive from Glasgow or 90 minutes by train.

COOKING CLASSES

The **Cook School Glasgow** (tel: 0845-166 6060; www.tennentstrainingacademy.co.uk/cookschool) at Tennent's in Duke Street offers even the most hopeless cooks a chance to learn how to bring food together in a tasty and attractive way. Choose from an afternoon course in Italian cookery (learning how to make gnocchi and delicious sauces among other dishes), up to a full-day masterclass preparing and cooking seafood.

NATURE

The National Trust for Scotland's **Thistle Camps** (www.nts.org.uk/ThistleCamps) recruit volunteers to repair upland and lowland footpaths, control rhododendron growth and erect fencing. You can even learn how to restore bogs in the estates and properties of the NTS, which include the likes of Ben Lawers, Ben Lomond and Brodick Castle in Arran. A week's volunteering includes basic accommodation and food.

Learn to play the most Scottish instrument of all at the College of Piping.

Practical Information

GETTING THERE

By air

Glasgow has an excellent international airport to the west at Abbotsinch (tel: 0844-481 5555), which is served by flights from all main UK airports and has connections to Europe and North America. It has direct motorway links to the city centre, a journey of about 15 minutes. A taxi to the city centre costs around £20 from a rank outside the terminal building. Glasgow Airport Shuttle Service 500 buses (24 hours, 364 days a year), which cost £6.50 one way and £9 return, connect with Glasgow Central (15 mins) and Buchanan Bus Station (25 mins). The Paisley Gilmour Street Railway Station is closest to the airport; around eight trains an hour depart for the city centre.

British Airways (tel: 0844-493 0887; www.britishairways.com) operates shuttle flights from Heathrow and Gatwick. Flybe (tel: 0371-700 2000; www.flybe.com) has flights from Belfast and Manchester. Easyjet (tel: 0330-365 5000; www.easyjet.com) connects Glasgow with Stansted, Luton and Gatwick, as well as Bristol, Belfast and Paris Charles de Gaulle, in France. Ryanair (tel: 0844-545 6524; www.ryanair.com) operates from Stansted to Glasgow International. There are also direct flights available to various other UK, European and North American destinations. For details of flights, and to book tickets online, visit www.glasgowairport.com.

Black taxi by the Stock Exchange building.

By car

From the south, the west-coast route follows the M1 to Birmingham, then the M6 to the Scottish border, then the A74 and M74, which joins the M8 into the city. The slower east-coast route follows the M1 and A1 into Edinburgh, then the cross-country M8 to Glasgow. From the north, the A9 joins the M9 near Stirling and then the M80, A80 and M8 into Glasgow.

By coach

National Express (tel: 08717-818 178; www.nationalexpress.com) runs a regular coach service from all points in England and Wales into Buchanan Bus Station.

By rail

Virgin Trains (tel: 0333-103 1031; www.virgintrains.co.uk) currently operates the main west-coast route from London, Birmingham and Manchester, but the running of the franchise will be up for negotiation again in 2017. Queen Street Station has a shuttle to Edinburgh and serves the north. For

In the subway.

general rail enquiries in Glasgow and Scotland: tel: 0344-811 0141; www.scotrail.co.uk. Buy tickets online at www.thetrainline.com.

GETTING AROUND

On foot

A colour-coded sign system facilitates navigation of the city centre and main visitor areas. Distinctive blue panels provide directions and information about sights, maps and pedestrian routes. The Glasgow VisitScotland Information Centre on Buchanan Street (see page 123) has decent free maps and some more detailed ones for a few pounds. Also available to download is the Glasgow Walking app developed by Glasgow City Council.

By public transport

Glasgow's subway network is one of the oldest in the world, but 15 stations on two 24-minute circular tracks, one clockwise and one anti-clockwise, mean that no journey will take longer than 12 minutes (www.spt.co.uk). Packages are available, such as the Family Day Tripper Tickets (unlimited travel on Scotrail services, subway, some ferries and many bus operators). A single ticket costs £1.40. The subway's 'All-Day' ticket is good value: for £4 you can enjoy one day's unlimited travel after 9am Monday to Friday and all day weekends. Above ground, Scotrail (www.scotrail.co.uk) runs the extensive rail network. Glasgow Central Station serves the South and England, while Queen Street Station handles trains to and from Edinburgh and the north. City Sightseeing Glasgow (www.citysightseeingglasgow.co.uk) runs open-air bus tours from George Square West. National Express, Citylink and Megabus coach companies operate out of Buchanan Street Bus Station.

Car hire and parking

Glasgow city-centre traffic is heavy, but a car is useful for excursions to outlying areas. Car-hire firms in Glasgow include: **Arnold Clark** (tel: 0141-954

Cycling

There are great cycle paths, including the 20-mile (32km) Glasgow to Loch Lomond Cycleway, from Bell's Bridge, beside the Clyde Auditorium on the Clyde, to Balloch. Bikes are carried free on all Strathclyde Passenger Transport-supported rail services. For information on cycle routes, visit www.sustrans.org.uk, tel: 0845-113 0065, or ask for the *Clyde and Loch Lomond Cycleway* leaflet at the tourist office.

The cycle path along Loch Katrine.

1962), **Avis** (tel: 0844-544 6064) and **Enterprise** (tel: 0141-221 2124).

Car parks are plentiful but busy, with spaces around St Enoch Square usually filled by mid-morning. Multi-storey car parks are at Mitchell Street, Cambridge Street, Waterloo Street, Cadogan Square, Concert Square, Oswald Street and Buchanan Galleries. Unauthorised parking is not advisable, as tow-away trucks and clamping units abound. If your accommodation is in the West End, take the subway into the city centre.

Steamer and seaplane

The world's last surviving paddle steamer, the PS *Waverley* (tel: 0845-130 4647), makes its home berth at Pacific Quay by the Glasgow Science Centre. A relic of the great days of steam, its massive engines are still open for inspection on summer cruises down the Firth of Clyde to Rothesay, Arran and the Kyles of Bute (www.waverleyexcursions.co.uk).

For a breathtaking flight over Loch Lomond, Tobermory, Oban and the west coast, charter a Loch Lomond Seaplane (tel: 01436-675 030; www.lochlomondseaplanes.com). Planes take off from the shore of Loch Lomond, 1 mile (2km) north of Balloch.

Lock Lomond seaplane.

One of the last surviving police boxes on Buchanan Street.

Taxis

Black taxis are licensed by Glasgow City Council and can be flagged down in the street, but there are also many private taxi firms, which are slightly cheaper.

FACTS FOR THE VISITOR

Disabled travellers

The Glasgow VisitScotland Information Centre dispenses advice and leaflets for disabled travellers. The city's main sights have improved provision and access in recent years. For information on disabled access regarding hotels and other businesses, consult www.disabledgo.com.

Emergencies

Fire, **Police**, **Ambulance**: tel: 999

Fire HQ: (north of the river) Port Dundas Road, tel: 0141-302 3111; (south of the river) McFarlane Street, tel: 0141-552 8222

Strathclyde Police HQ: 173 Pitt Street, tel: 0141-532 2000

Royal Infirmary: Castle Street, tel: 0141-211 4000

Western Infirmary: Dumbarton Road, tel: 0141-211 2000

Opening hours

City centre shops are generally open 9am–5.30pm (Mon–Sat). Many stores stay open later – some until 8pm – on a Thursday. Sunday opening is now common in the city centre: noon–5pm is the norm.

Most major banks open 9.30am–4.30pm weekdays; some open Saturday mornings until 12.30pm.

Postal services

Most post offices are open Monday to Friday 9am to 5.30pm, and Saturday 9am to 12.30–1pm. The branch at 177 Sauchiehall Street is open on a Sunday, 10.30am–2.30pm. For help and advice on all post office counter services, tel: 08457-223 344; www.postoffice.co.uk.

Tourist information

The **Glasgow VisitScotland Information Centre**, 10 Sauchiehall Street (tel: 0845 859 1006; www.visitscotland.com; Apr–Sept Mon–Sat 9am–6pm, Sun 10am–5pm, Oct–Mar 9am–6pm, all year Sun noon–4pm), provides practical guidance on getting around the city and the surrounding areas. Staff are on hand to help with information on the vast range of tours available, the city's historical and cultural attractions, as well as providing an accommodation booking service. There's also a small shop on site. For further information, see also www.peoplemakeglasgow.com.

Bureaux de change can be found at Travelex (Glasgow International Airport), **ICE** (66 Gordon Street, tel: 0203-437 0744) and **Thomas Cook** (15–17 Gordon Street, tel: 0844-335 7296).

Crowds at the busy Queen Street train station.

Gay and Lesbian Scene

Glasgow has a thriving gay scene and is home to Scotland's Pride Glasgow 2-day festival in the summer (weekend July/Aug dates vary; www.pride.scot). Popular gay-lesbian hangouts are centred on the Merchant City and include **Delmonica's** (68 Virginia Street; tel: 0141-552 4803) for food, cabaret and club nights; Speakeasy (10 John Street; tel: 0845-166 6036) for cocktails and DJs; and **Underground Bar** (6a John Street; tel: 0141-553 2456), a stylish place big on home-cooked food and friendliness. For more information and latest listings check out www.glasgow.gaycities.com.

Girls' night out.

Accommodation

Glasgow's hotels range from the swanky and expensive to cosy B&Bs housed in handsome Victorian houses. A plethora of boutique hotels – some contemporary-style new-builds and others imaginative conversions of historic buildings – have revitalised accommodation options in Glasgow and have upped the standards generally. The Glasgow VisitScotland Information Centre (see page 123) provides an accommodation booking service.

Prices of hotels listed here vary seasonally; the ranges below (quoted as a guide only) suggest prices for one night in a double room on a bed-and-breakfast basis in peak season:

££££ = over £180
£££ = £120–180
££ = £80–120
£ = under £80

CENTRAL GLASGOW AND MERCHANT CITY

ABode Glasgow

129 Bath Street; tel: 0141-221 6789; www.abodehotels.co.uk.

Located in an elegant Edwardian Bath Street building, which once housed the atmospheric Arthouse Hotel, this hotel reflects the city's modern renaissance, beautifully combining traditional features with boutique design and modern comforts. *££*

Brunswick Hotel

106–8 Brunswick Street; tel: 0141-552 0001; www.brunswickhotel.co.uk.

In the heart of the Merchant City quarter, this stylish hotel is extremely good value in terms of both location and elegance. There's also an on-site Italian café-cum-restaurant. *££*

Hotel du Vin at One Devonshire Gardens

1 Devonshire Gardens, Great Western Road; tel: 0141-339 2001; www.hotelduvin.com.

Luxury accommodation in an elegant tree-lined terrace comprising five sandstone houses. Quality and comfort abound, from the Egyptian cotton bedding to the whisky snug, cigar shack and award-winning eatery. *£££*

Radisson Blu Hotel

301 Argyle Street; tel: 0141-204 3333; www.radissonblu.co.uk/hotel-glasgow.

Around the corner from Glasgow Central Station, this hotel has a jaw-dropping glass-fronted lobby that will impress anyone interested in contemporary design. The cavernous art-filled atrium bar is a social hub, while the Collage bar and restaurant has picked up awards. Standard modern rooms can seem a tad dull, but the corner suites are gorgeous. *££££*

A truly luxurious bathing experience at the Hotel du Vin at One Devonshire Gardens.

The stylish bar at ABode Glasgow.

WEST END AND BY THE CLYDE

Alamo Guest House

46 Gray Street, Kelvingrove; tel: 0141-339 2395; www.alamoguesthouse.com.

A popular family-run hotel opposite Kelvingrove Park set in a grand terraced house. The cosy rooms are simply furnished, well maintained and offer great value. ££

Crowne Plaza Glasgow

Congress Road; tel: 0871-423 4896; www.ihg.com/crowneplaza.

Modern high-rise beside the Clyde and the SECC, offering a range of functional rooms and suites, a grand reception with bar-restaurant and shop, and a pool. ££

Hilton Garden Inn

Finnieston Quay; tel: 0141-240 1002; http://hiltongardeninn3.hilton.com.

A stylish yet comfortable place to stay next to the Clyde, with a fresh contemporary design and beguiling café-bar with views of the river from the terrace. Free Wi-fi in every room. ££

Kelvin Hotel

15 Buckingham Terrace; tel: 0141-339 7143; www.kelvinhotel.com.

Family-owned hotel in an impressive Victorian building in the West End. Decorated in soft pastels, the guest rooms have high ceilings and free Wi-fi. A fully fitted communal kitchen is available to guests. £

Village Urban Resort

7 Festival Gate, Pacific Quay; tel: 0871-964 7000; www.village-hotels.co.uk.

Opened in 2015, this resort offers everything you could want under one roof – at extremely good value. The very on-trend bedrooms feature super-comfy beds. Other facilities include an indoor pool, gym and pub dining. £

SOUTHSIDE

Glasgow Guest House

56 Dumbrek Road, near Pollok Park; tel: 0141-427 0129; www.glasgow-guest-house.co.uk.

This bed and breakfast offers homely accommodation and is handy for the parks detailed in Tour 8 (see page 86) and the airport. £

Mar Hall Golf and Spa Resort

Earl of Mar Estate, Bishopton, Renfrew; tel: 0141-812 9999; www.marhall.com.

Stunning Gothic mansion within acres of woodland and with an 18-hole golf course, just 10 minutes west of Glasgow airport. Luxury rooms and suites come in calming hues. The Decléor Spa offers treatments and a swimming pool. ££££

Number 10
10–16 Queen's Drive; tel: 0141-424 0160; www.10hotel.co.uk.
In a great location with views over Queen's Park, this graceful Victorian building has stylish interiors that fluently combine fashionable design with original features. The chic restaurant offers classic cooking with a modern twist. *££*

Sherbrooke Castle Hotel
11 Sherbrooke Avenue, Pollokshields; tel: 0141-427 4227; www.sherbrookecastlehotel.co.uk.
A Victorian mock-Gothic pile complete with baronial turrets near Pollok Park. Tartan carpets, period furnishings and antiques give the public areas a cosy atmospheric feel, while guest rooms have modern bathrooms, warmth and free Wi-fi. *£££*

NORTH OF THE CITY

Cameron House Hotel
Loch Lomond; tel: 01389-755 565; www.qhotels.co.uk.
This five-star hotel is housed in a luxurious baronial-style mansion in a stunning Loch Lomond waterside setting. There are first-class spa and golf facilities, and you can even arrive by seaplane. *££££*

Dakota Eurocentral
1–3 Parklands Avenue, Eurocentral Business Park (off the A8/M8); tel: 01698-835 444; www.dakotahotels.co.uk
A stylish yet cosy hotel with lots of contemporary design touches and free Wi-fi. The award-winning bar and grill serves excellent Scottish fish dishes and a good range of cocktails. *££*

WEBSITES

For a comprehensive list of hotels in the city, see www.glasgowguide.co.uk/hotels.html.
Guesthouses/Bed & Breakfasts: www.information-britain.co.uk; www.scottishaccommodationindex.com; www.laterooms.com
Green: www.organicholidays.co.uk; www.ecofriendlytourist.com
Self-catering: For those staying for more than a few days, an apartment is a sensible option:
www.citybaseapartments.com; www.glasgowloftapartment.co.uk; www.max-servicedapartments.co.uk; www.dreamhouseapartments.com; www.hot-el-apartments.com

The pool at the Crowne Plaza Glasgow.

Index

Credits

Insight Guides Great Breaks Glasgow
Editor: Carine Tracanelli
Author: Ron Clark, Colin Hutchison, Nick Bruno
Head of Production: Rebeka Davies
Picture Editor: Tom Smyth
Cartography Update: Carte
Photo credits: Abode Hotels 125; Alamy 69B; Citizens Theatre Ltd 34T; Cornell Univeristy Library 10T; David Cruickshanks/Apa Publications 7T, 11, 25B, 28T, 29B, 41, 54B, 54T, 57T, 58B, 62, 64B, 123T; David Grinly 6MC; Douglas Macgilvray/Apa 6ML, 15, 16B, 21B, 32T, 35T, 42T, 58T, 71T, 73B, 84T, 97B; Dreamstime 7M, 75; Fotolia 117T; Getty Images 66TL, 67T; Glasgay! Festival/Eamonn McGoldrick 123B; Glasgow City Marketing Bureau 118T; Graeme Maclean 117B; Hunterian Museum and Art Gallery 80B, 81T, 81B, 82T; Ilpo Koskinen 60; iStock 7TR, 18B, 19T, 20T, 21T, 22, 25T, 37T, 38ML, 52B, 70T, 71B, 88T, 89T, 104TL, 104ML, 105T, 113, 118B, 119; Leonardo 124, 126; Library of Congress 52T; Mockford & Bonetti/Apa 4/5, 6MC, 6ML, 7MR, 7BR, 7M, 9, 9, 12T, 12B, 14, 16T, 17T, 17B, 18T, 19B, 20B, 23T, 23B, 24B, 24T, 26, 27, 28B, 29T, 30T, 30B, 31, 32B, 33T, 33B, 34B, 35B, 36B, 38TL, 40, 42B, 43B, 44B, 44T, 45, 47T, 46B, 47, 48, 49, 50, 51, 53T, 53B, 55T, 55B, 56, 57B, 61, 63T, 64T, 68, 69T, 70B, 72T, 72B, 73T, 74, 76T, 76B, 77, 78, 80T, 82B, 83T, 83B, 84B, 85, 86, 88B, 89B, 90T, 90B, 91T, 92T, 92B, 93, 94, 96T, 96B, 97T, 98T, 98B, 99, 100, 101, 103T, 102B, 103, 106, 107, 108T, 108B, 109, 110, 111, 112, 115, 116T, 116B, 120, 121T, 121B, 122T, 122B; Nesbit Wylie 63B; Pictures Colour Library 39T; Public domain 10B, 66ML; Stephen Thomas 91B; Tom Brogan 13; Ville.fi 43T
Cover credits: all images iStock

CONTACTING THE EDITORS:
Every effort has been made to provide accurate information in this publication, but changes are inevitable. The publisher cannot be responsible for any resulting loss, inconvenience or injury. We would appreciate it if readers would call our attention to any errors or outdated information. We also welcome your suggestions; please contact us at: hello@insightguides.com

Information has been obtained from sources believed to be reliable, but its accuracy and completeness, and the opinions based thereon, are not guaranteed.

Third Edition 2016

Printed in China by CTPS

Worldwide distribution enquiries:
APA Publications (Singapore) Pte, 7030 Ang Mo Kio Avenue 5, 08-65 Northstar @ AMK, Singapore 569880
apasin@singnet.com.sg
Distributed in the UK and Ireland by:
Dorling Kindersley Ltd, A Penguin Group company, 80 Strand, London, WC2R 0RL
sales@uk.dk.com
Distributed in the US by:
Ingram Publisher Services, 1 Ingram Boulevard, PO Box 3006, La Vergne, TN 37086-1986
ips@ingramcontent.com
Distributed in Australia and New Zealand by:
Woodslane, 10 Apollo St, Warriewood, NSW 2102, Australia
info@woodslane.com.au